teach®
yourself

how to run a
marathon

teach yourself®

how to run a
marathon
tim rogers

796. 4252

For UK order enquiries: please contact Bookpoint Ltd, 130 Milton Park, Abingdon, Oxon, OX14 4SB. Telephone: +44 (0) 1235 827720. Fax: +44 (0) 1235 400454. Lines are open 09.00–17.00, Monday to Saturday, with a 24-hour message answering service. Details about our titles and how to order are available at www.teachyourself.co.uk

For USA order enquiries: please contact McGraw-Hill Customer Services, PO Box 545, Blacklick, OH 43004-0545, USA. Telephone: 1-800-722-4726. Fax: 1-614-755-5645.

For Canada order enquiries: please contact McGraw-Hill Ryerson Ltd, 300 Water St, Whitby, Ontario, L1N 9B6, Canada. Telephone: 905 430 5000. Fax: 905 430 5020.

Long renowned as the authoritative source for self-guided learning – with more than 50 million copies sold worldwide – the **teach yourself** series includes over 500 titles in the fields of languages, crafts, hobbies, business, computing and education.

British Library Cataloguing in Publication Data: a catalogue record for this title is available from the British Library.

Library of Congress Catalog Card Number: on file.

First published in UK 1994 by Hodder Education, 338 Euston Road, London, NW1 3BH.

First published in US 1994 by The McGraw-Hill Companies, Inc.

This edition published 2006.

The **teach yourself** name is a registered trade mark of Hodder Headline.

Copyright © 2006 Tim Rogers

Typeset by Transet Limited, Coventry, England.
Printed in Great Britain for Hodder Education, a division of Hodder Headline, 338 Euston Road, London, NW1 3BH, by Cox & Wyman Ltd, Reading, Berkshire.

The publisher has used its best endeavours to ensure that the URLs for external websites referred to in this book are correct and active at the time of going to press. However, the publisher and the author have no responsibility for the websites and can make no guarantee that a site will remain live or that the content will remain relevant, decent or appropriate.

Hodder Headline's policy is to use papers that are natural, renewable and recyclable products and made from wood grown in sustainable forests. The logging and manufacturing processes are expected to conform to the environmental regulations of the country of origin.

Impression number   10 9 8 7 6 5 4 3 2 1
Year   2010 2009 2008 2007 2006

contents

acknowledgements

Writing this book has been a fascinating experience and one that would have been much more difficult without the support of my partner Lisa Frost, who remained patient and supportive throughout even when my office door seemed permanently locked. To everyone at realbuzz.com who helped in the editing stages, to the staff at Hodder and to the London Marathon team a very big thank you. To my son Sam who collects and then loses my marathon memorabilia, hopefully when you're a bit older you'll experience what is like to cross the marathon finish line for the first time. And to everyone who has been on one of my training days thanks for your feedback!

Thanks also to my parents who drove me to my half marathon debut many, many years ago telling me throughout the journey that it wasn't too late to pull out – might this book get you running?

Tim Rogers

Running a marathon is one of the toughest physical challenges that you will ever take on, but one that with the right support and guidance is very achievable.

Every April, thousands of people tackle the Flora London Marathon, many of them running a marathon for the very first time. They get to the finish line through a combination of determination, guts and knowledge, the latter coming in many cases from listening to those that have been there before.

This book gives you a head start. Tim Rogers has been a regular London Marathon runner for many years and has trained thousands of runners, helping many to complete the marathon in London and at other famous marathon courses. In this book you will find everything you need to prepare yourself for one of the biggest days of your life, with training, nutrition and injury advice as well as fundraising tips should you decide to join the thousands of others who raise much-needed funds for charity.

Written in a friendly but informative style, *Teach yourself to run a marathon* also contains useful background information on such things as the importance of friends and family in your training. Virtually everyone who trains for their first marathon needs the support of those closest to them and without it this event can be even tougher. There is also plenty on preparing yourself mentally. Marathon training isn't just about preparing your body, it is also about your mind. The stronger you are mentally, the easier you will find the long, hard months of training and the easier you will find race day.

When the winter weather becomes too much during your training, you may feel that the gym is a better option, and if that's the case you will find a chapter on how to get the most from your time indoors. Many marathon runners every year combine running on a treadmill with road running, and also use the stationary bike and rowing machine to great effect as they prepare for their big day. Cross training is becoming more and more popular and this book explains why.

If you think you need to hear from a first timer then don't worry, that is also covered. Sue Thearle, a BBC TV sports presenter, tackled the Flora London Marathon in 2005 and supported her husband as he repeated the act in 2006. You will find the diary of an absolute beginner a great insight into what it's really like to go from dreaming about completing this great race to walking away from the finish area with the famous medal around your neck.

Armed with the knowledge that you'll find in this book, all you've got to do now, of course, is to make sure that you add the guts and determination!

See you in April ...

David Bedford

Race Director
Flora London Marathon

01

are you up to it?

In this chapter you will learn:
- that marathon training takes time
- that you need a lot of mental strength
- that friends and family are crucial.

Tip at the top

Be prepared to make major lifestyle changes and make sure that the closest to you totally support your efforts.

Running a marathon is an idea that far more people entertain than was the case a few years ago. Even as recently as the 1990s, if you said to a friend that you were considering it, you would be met with an expression that indicated you were a little sad and should perhaps think about something with a little more credibility. It simply wasn't trendy. Now it is, and how!

Applications to run the Flora London Marathon have increased dramatically in the last five years, culminating in record numbers for the 25th anniversary event in 2005. It now seems that the marathon is on the list of 'must do' activities, like a bungee jump, or scuba diving. It's one of those things that you have to do by the time you are thirty or forty; a life stage activity and a social event rolled into one.

Its credibility may have changed, but the distance hasn't and this, unfortunately, is the stumbling block for many people. Running a marathon isn't easy, but because more and more people are taking on the challenge there is a perception that it might all be a little bit easier than it used to be. It isn't. What have changed are people's finish-time expectations and it is this that has made it all seem different. Now it's acceptable to do a six-hour marathon, whereas ten years ago it wasn't. A four-hour marathon is almost perceived to be world-record pace. The emphasis has changed, especially in London, and it is now on raising money for charity rather than fast times. While this is ultimately a good thing, particularly for the beneficiaries, it has potentially made the challenge seem a little less severe as finish-time expectations are lower. Be warned – it will be hard whatever finish time you are going for, which brings us to the leading question, 'Are you up to it?'

It's important before embarking on the whole marathon experience, and that includes the initial application, to appreciate exactly what is involved. If you are an absolute beginner or have some distant fitness experience from a few years back, you can do it, but you will need to give yourself six to nine months in order to prepare properly. If you are running a couple of times a week, totalling around ten miles, then you need to give yourself four to six months. It will hurt, but then anything that is a real challenge will hurt, or it wouldn't be one in the first place. The sense of achievement will be enormous, but there will be plenty of days during the training programme when you will feel like packing it all in. If you keep going and see it through you will have one of the most memorable days of your life. If you embark on the training but then give up you will have denied yourself one of the most incredible sporting experiences out there. But what exactly is involved?

Time

There are no short cuts when it comes to training for a marathon. You will need to spend time training, no matter what level you are at now and what your aspirations are for race day. Training is all about 'time on feet' (we'll come back to this in the training chapter). The more time you spend on your feet, the more you will enjoy your big day. If you don't commit the time to your training you will have a thoroughly miserable race day and potentially not even finish.

So what sort of time do you need to allocate to your marathon experience? Putting the actual training aside for now, there are plenty of issues to consider that will all eat into your life. Planning your training and your build-up schedule, entering events, driving to them, and so on. Training for a marathon involves more than just the training. There are plenty of other things to consider. You should allocate around *four or five hours* a week to the planning and administrative side of preparing for a marathon, and that's if you don't have to worry about fundraising.

If you have a guaranteed charity entry for the Flora London Marathon, for example, or you have your own place but are running still for charity, then you've got the fundraising to add to your preparation time. A guaranteed charity place will require higher levels of fundraising as you will have entered into a contract with the charity to raise a pre-agreed sum of money (normally around £1500–£2000). Do not underestimate the amount of time you will need to spend fundraising if you have to raise that sum of money – for now allocate around *five hours* a week. We will cover fundraising in depth in its own chapter.

So, on to the training. Depending on the time you are hoping to achieve on your big day you will start off running three times a week and build up to five or maybe six. Your early runs during the week will be very short, but at the weekend they will always be longer. As you get nearer the event the long run will be well over two hours and often nearer three. Add on to that everything that goes with a run – psyching yourself up, getting changed and then stretched and showered afterwards – and you are looking at around five hours. An average run will obviously be a lot less than that but in most cases, with everything that goes with it, you will be looking at around an hour at the start of your programme and an hour and a half as things progress. Averaging this out you will need to commit at least five hours a week from the start for your training – that includes the preparation time and 15 to 20 hours as you get into the last month. That is a lot of time and it has to come from somewhere. Be realistic as to where it is coming from. Hopefully from time spent watching the TV!

Add all this up and you could well be looking at around ten hours a week in the early days, up to well over 30 as you progress. It will all be well worth it come your big day!

Mental strength

You will need this in bucket loads, for lots of reasons!

The weather

If you're running an autumn marathon and you're based in the northern hemisphere then most of your training will be over the summer months. This is a real bonus as not only is the temperature much better but you have long nights for your training, which can make the world of difference. If, however, you are planning on running in London in April then it's a different world.

Training through the winter provides many challenges, among which rain, freezing temperatures and constantly running in the dark are only three. This is not said to put anyone off, just to alert you to the fact that if London is your goal you need to face up to running in less than clement weather on many, many occasions. This is where you will need the first of these bucketfuls of mental strength.

There will be countless times when you know you have to go for a run, you open the door and you look out on bleak conditions that are fit for no-one, least of all runners. You must go. Do not think of backing out, unless conditions are dangerous and that is not very often the case. You need to blank out thoughts of giving into conditions, unless there is a case of injury and then you should go to the gym and use the treadmill as an alternative. If you start to let the conditions get the better of you then your training plan will become useless. You will get further and further behind and your morale will drop. You need to be strong and fight the temptation to shut the door before you've even gone through it!

Tiredness

As your body adapts to the rigours of the training plan, so it will go through a series of changes that prepare it for the challenge that lies ahead. Inevitably it will make you tired, particularly in the early stages, and it will be extremely tempting to miss a few sessions because you feel too exhausted. Here again, just like the weather issue, you must be prepared to fight this temptation. It is another mind over matter problem.

The training plans have all been written in a way that incorporates these body adaptations and there are plenty of rest days that give you a chance to recover. Clearly, if you feel you really do need another day to rest then you must do so, but don't take too many. Quite often it is the rigours of our work days that make us feel too tired to run, rather than the effects of the training plan itself. Another bucketful of mental strength is needed to get home from work, change into your running gear and get back outside for a run. Don't leave it until you've had your main meal, as it will be another hour or two after that until it has been fully digested and it's safe to run. By then it could be ten or eleven at night and that isn't the best time to be out running. If you get in from work and feel you haven't got enough energy to go straight out then grab a quick snack like a bowl of cereal, banana or energy bar.

There is always something better to do!

The final bucketful of mental strength is saved for the biggest problem of all: there always seems to be something better or more interesting to do. Your favourite TV programmes, seeing friends, having a drink down the local – anything can seem better than going for a run pretty much most of the time! You really do have to tackle this problem head on and as early as possible.

If you are addicted to a particular soap opera and it happens to be shown at the optimum running time (and it probably will be!) then you will probably have to rely on family or friends to let you know what's happening or watch the omnibus episode later in the week. You cannot be a slave to TV during your training – your running must come first!

If you visit friends at a certain time each week and it happens to be the best time to run, then again you should move it. The same goes for that regular drink – move it to another time.

Your mental strength should come in part from the knowledge that it isn't for long and then you can go back to your old ways, if of course you want to. Be focused and put that regular run ahead of other things that can easily be moved. Some can't be moved, but the majority can and it is these that must give way. Be strong and dig deep when temptation strikes!

Commitment

To run a marathon you will need to show real commitment, both to yourself and others. Are you able to do this?

Taking on a challenge of this magnitude, especially if you are a novice runner, requires a level of commitment that is far higher than you might expect. There are so many different facets to the whole process, from beginning to end, that you need to be aware of exactly what is required. Importantly, it's not just about you, it's about a lot of others besides.

Commitment to your training

The training plan (and the events that form an important part of it) is the key component of your marathon training. Follow it and you will get to the finish line in the time predicted. Veer from it and you may not. You must be committed from day one to this plan and regard it as your bible for the next four or five months. It has been designed with your specific requirements in mind and you must stick to it. This is your commitment to yourself and it must be your number one priority. This is you being selfish.

It is this selfishness that is a critical component of your training. Most of us are not naturally selfish, but to successfully complete a marathon we all have to develop a selfish streak, whether we like it or not. We'll look at the importance of commitment to others shortly, but it is the commitment to yourself and your goal that is more important than any other. Without selfishness you will not succeed in your quest to complete a marathon. You have to have a singular focus throughout the months of training that will at times almost change your personality. Mental strength, commitment and all the other ingredients that you need could well make you a more determined person than you have ever been. You will find other personal goals and challenges easier after this one and will feel very differently about yourself when faced with situations that may previously have proved daunting to you.

Commit to yourself and your training and you will succeed.

Commitment to friends and family

For all of the talk about the selfish streak that you'll need, you also need to remain committed to your friends and family. While undoubtedly there will be occasions when you will upset them for one reason or another (probably because you can't go out on a Saturday with the family due to the long run, or you can't meet friends for a drink after work because you have to hit the streets for a five-mile run), you need to remember that they do play an important part in the whole process. It's a case of balance.

Balance is a vital part of life in whatever you are doing and it has even greater significance when it comes to marathon training. It is easy to become obsessive when it comes to running and if you do then inevitably it is those around you that will suffer. Don't let that happen – make sure you look after those who you'll need as times get tougher and who you will definitely want to be around come race day. Work together and compromise; don't lose sight of their importance to you.

Commitment to your charity

If you are running for a charity then this is another group who will need your commitment. If you're not running for charity then maybe you should think about it. It will make the whole experience even more worthwhile.

More and more charities in the UK, and to a lesser extent overseas, are becoming increasingly dependant on running events as key fundraising vehicles. They are generally adding more runs to their supported events list each year and are seeing higher returns from individuals per event and across the sector as a whole. They are funding research and treatment programmes from revenue from running events, so if you say you are going to run for a specific charity and have given an indication as to the amount you hope to raise, then it is quite likely that this will have been included in a future cash-flow forecast and there will be numerous people who are now relying on you to deliver.

This reliance on the runner is especially significant with what is known in the trade as 'guaranteed-place' runners as opposed to 'own-place' runners. The former are places in running events, such as the London and New York marathons, that the charities have bought from the organizers. The runner makes a commitment to the charity that they will raise a pre-agreed amount of money in return for the place (see Chapter 02 on getting a place). The charity is depending on this money and there could be budgetary implications if you don't raise the amount that you've promised. Own-place runners, on the other hand, are more of a bonus to the charity although they will forecast an amount for each event and will budget accordingly. The perfect scenario for a charity is to recruit more own-place than planned runners and for each to raise more than expected. Own-place cost the charity much less than a guaranteed-place runner, so if you do get a place in an event directly from the organizers then contact a charity and raise funds for them – they will really appreciate it.

Once you have said that you will run for a charity, either on a guaranteed place or as an own-place runner, then this is where the third form of commitment begins. For everybody's sake, including the charity fundraising manager and the people who are dependant on the charity for research, treatment or counselling, do not let them down. You must be as committed to the charity as you are to yourself. Regard the fundraising as being as important as your training – they are not mutually exclusive. Chapter 10 focuses on fundraising and suggests many ways that you can help to raise money. Read it as thoroughly as you do the training plans. Even if you're lucky enough to be an own-place runner in an event like the Flora London Marathon, don't forget that once you say you are going to run for a particular charity then it will start to incur costs. These include the costs of all the postal correspondence, running packs, training days, email services and running vests. An average own-place runner can cost a charity between £50 and £100. If you say you're going to run for them and submit nothing then you will have cost the charity that amount of money, and no-one wants that on their conscience. Not only will you have they cost the charity these maintenance costs, but the charity has also had to pay for the place. Worst of all, someone else will have been refused a place and they may well have raised many thousands. Hundreds of charities up and down the length of Britain want you to run for their worthy cause, but once you've agreed to it they also want and need your commitment.

The secret is to start your fundraising early and have it uppermost in your thoughts from the minute you sign up, right up until race day.

Lifestyle changes

In addition to the need for time, mental strength and commitment, you also need to add lifestyle changes to the list. There is a separate chapter on this important area of marathon training and preparation, but at this stage it is important to stress that you will have to make some changes to the way that you live if you are to get through the challenge that lies ahead.

Depending on how you currently live your life, some of you will need to make more changes than others. There is the need for a good sleep pattern, a balanced diet, time, the training itself and the potential changes these things will make to your social life, which clearly will be greater in some cases than others.

Getting the recommended eight hours of sleep a night becomes even more important when you have such physical demands as running a marathon. The training will take a great deal out of you and it essential that you give your body plenty of rest and adequate sleep. If you have a hectic social life with many late nights then you will need to make some changes. Burning the candle at both ends will simply not work when you have to prepare for probably the biggest physical challenge of your life. You cannot deprive yourself of sleep and expect to get through the training programme in a manner which will do you justice on race day. You may finish but you probably won't enjoy it.

Your diet will inevitably change and it will include a large percentage of carbohydrates, which we'll cover in more detail later. You will grow to hate (or love, potentially) rice, potatoes and especially pasta, which all form an essential part of a runner's diet. You may choose to reduce your dairy intake if you find, as many runners do, that they develop intolerance to dairy products as they do more training, and you will have to cut back on your alcohol consumption. You won't have to cut it out completely, just take it easy during your training period, with definitely no seriously heavy nights! Big, alcohol-fuelled nights can take a long time to recover from and you will not have that time available, especially as you get further into your training programme. It's only for a few months and you may well find that actually you feel so much healthier because of it that you take a different approach to alcohol in the future. Fatty foods are another vice that you will need to cut back on. They take a long time for your body to process and ultimately add very little of value. All of these changes will make you feel better in their own right, but add the training to them and they will fundamentally alter how you feel about yourself.

Making time for your running, and the potential changes to your social life as a result, are covered at the start of this chapter, but together with a good sleep pattern and adjustments to your diet they constitute some fundamental changes to how you live your life that will make running a marathon difficult for many people. They are all, in reality, changes that most of the population could benefit from but for many, particularly those at a certain life stage, they are changes that are simply not practicable.

So, after reading about all the challenges and the changes that you may need to make to successfully complete your marathon challenge – are you up to it? Are you able to find the time, develop the mental strength and give everyone, including yourself, the commitment to take it on? Can you make the necessary lifestyle adjustments to make it all happen?

If you can't then there is always next year – although don't put it off forever, but if you can then welcome to one of the most rewarding sports around. The feeling of satisfaction when you cross the marathon finish line for the first time is indescribable, particularly at one of the big city-centre events, and the feeling the second, third, fourth times … is pretty much the same. If you want a challenge in your life then you have found it. Read on, you won't regret it.

02

choosing your first marathon and getting a place

In this chapter you will learn:
- how to enter your first marathon
- which are the top marathon events
- how to run for charity.

Tip at the top

For your first marathon, choose one where you will get plenty of crowd support. Choose one of the World Marathon Majors.

Where do you begin? Where should your first marathon be? There are literally hundreds of marathons around the world, including some of the most unlikely destinations such as Antarctica, the North Pole, Mongolia, the Great Wall of China and Beirut. The US boasts a marathon in virtually every city and a wide selection in most states, so wherever you want to run a marathon there is a pretty good chance that you will be able to. It's never been easier to find your ideal marathon destination either. A few minutes surfing the Internet and you will have a list of your top ten, with most of them having detailed websites, full of everything that you need to know.

How you get a place very much depends on the type of race that you want to enter. The smaller marathons are pretty easy to get into, whereas the bigger city-centre marathons are often more difficult, but very much worth the effort.

Where should you run?

First you need to decide what type of marathon you want to run. There are a number of differences in marathons around the world and the choice of your first one could be a deciding factor in whether you come back for another! Where you run is probably one of the most important decisions in your running career. Plenty of blossoming potential careers have gone nowhere because the wrong decision was made about the all-important first marathon. Think about exactly what you are trying to get out of your first marathon. What are you hoping to achieve and how are you going to achieve it?

When choosing your first marathon you should consider a number of different factors that will all have a major bearing on how much you enjoy the race. Is the course flat? What are the facilities like? Is it easy to get to? Where are you going to stay? How many others are going to be running? How many people will be watching? Are there plenty of vantage points for your friends and family and can they move around the course easily?

What's the support package like from the organizers? Do you get a medal and/or goody bag at the end of the race as a memento of your efforts?

When you've considered the answers to these and other questions then you are ready to choose your first marathon, which of course should be many months before the big day itself. Don't leave this decision until the last minute. You should think long and hard about this important choice, preferably a year or so in advance. Running a marathon, particularly if you choose an overseas event, takes a lot of planning and you should leave nothing to chance. There are a number of good international calendars on the Internet, including the one on realbuzz.com. These give you the dates, website addresses and contact details so you can research easily online what's available. You should compare and contrast each of your short-listed events and match them to the answers of the questions above. Once you have decided which one to go for then it's time to enter.

Entering your first marathon

Generally speaking, most marathons have got a decent website and most have online entry. If they don't, like the Flora London Marathon, there will be a very good reason why they don't. Entering online is extremely easy and is becoming increasingly popular. Those events that do offer online entry have seen the percentage of this against paper entry rise dramatically in recent years and in many cases is 80 per cent of the total. Once on the relevant section of the event's website you simply complete the required information and pay via a secure section of the site using your credit card. If your entry is accepted it will be confirmed via email.

Some marathons also have a postal entry form that you can ask for if you prefer not to use your credit card online, and others have a downloadable version of the entry form on the website. When you send your form to the organizers remember to enclose a stamped, addressed envelope with your application, if requested. Some small races operate on a tight budget and these measures help keep costs down. In most cases you will know if your entry has been received by the cashing of your cheque.

The next time that you'll hear from the organizers is likely to be the receipt of race-day instructions and your race number.

They all communicate with their runners in different ways and some will require you to go to a pre-race exhibition to collect your number, but the general approach is a letter a few weeks beforehand that contains all you need to know for the big day.

However, the big boys of the marathon world can be very, very different.

The Flora London Marathon, one of the world's best marathons, is one of these big boys. It's definitely not a case of 'fill in the entry form' and you're in; it's more a case of 'I'll try the public ballot first and try other options if I don't get in that way'.

This is because events like this are extremely popular. They have many more applications for places than they have places available and in order to make sure that everyone has a fair chance of getting in they operate a ballot entry system. There is a date by which you must get your application in – usually the middle of October for London – and then a period of waiting until you find out if you have been successful in getting a place. If you have got in, your focus then needs to turn to your training and if you haven't then it turns to alternative entry options, the most obvious one being the charity option.

The World Marathon Majors

The five biggest and best marathons around the world have now joined forces and created the World Marathon Majors. If you are deciding on your first marathon then make it one of these. Berlin, London, New York, Boston and Chicago offer marathons that no first timer should miss. They are like no others and have organizational standards and crowd support at such levels that you cannot fail to be overwhelmed as you cross the finish line. Other cities also have big events, but these five are unparalleled.

From the moment you enter the event to the moment you cross the finish line you will see why these events stand out in the marathon world. All-year-round planning ensures that the standard of all aspects of the runner's experience is high, including the all-important communication. Email newsletters, high-tech websites, event magazines, state of the art expos and virtually instant results make these marathons unmissable. When you run these events you will understand why so many before you have worked hard to get a place. The organization on the day and the unbelievable crowd support ensure that the time you spend running will be some of the most unforgettable of your life.

As you can imagine, as a result of these incredibly high standards it is not easy to get a place in these events. They all operate slightly different entry systems, with some rewarding runners who are quick off the mark. In Berlin and Chicago there is an online entry programme on a first come, first served basis. For both events there is a three- or four-month window and if you enter during this period then you will get a place. Check the event websites for the relevant launch dates and get in quickly. Every year they close when the entry limit is reached and this gets earlier each year. Boston has entry qualification and if you hit their standards then you will get a place. New York and London have ballots and they are very difficult to get into. If you are a UK runner the best way to get in is often through the charities who have guaranteed places.

Running for charity

Gone are the days where the leading charities had a handful of runners in ill-fitting vests raising a few hundred pounds – it has all changed. Now the biggest charities have teams of 500 or more in the Flora London Marathon, with a target of over £1 million being attainable. Charities of all sizes now look to events like this as a key part of revenue generation for the future and are encouraging as many runners as possible to join their teams. But how does it all work?

The biggest and most successful events that are over subscribed each year keep a number of places aside and sell them direct to the charities. The charities then recruit runners who commit to raising a certain amount of sponsorship. This sponsorship will cover the cost of the place, the administration involved and leave some 'profit' that the charity can then invest back to help achieve its goals. It is a 'win, win' situation, with everyone benefiting from the arrangement. Don't think that it's just a case of saying, 'I'll have a place' and you're in. It's very different now from how it was a few years ago.

Most of the charities receive hundreds of applications each year for their London Marathon 'charity places' and they can now be very selective when deciding who gets one. Each charity has a clear set of guidelines that they use when allocating these places, including an assessment of how good they think the applicant's fundraising potential is. Be realistic when forecasting how much you think you can raise and don't tell them a figure that you think they want to hear. If it is unrealistic then don't suggest it as it could come back to haunt you a few months later! Also remember that the charities build their budgets around projections of sponsorship from these events so don't be unfair to them by giving them false information. Remember that if you are accepted by a charity for one of its places then you are entering into a 'contract' with it and you are obliged to raise the agreed level of sponsorship for it. Even if you got your own place in an event like the Flora London Marathon, rather than a 'charity place', you should still think about trying to raise sponsorship funds anyway. There are a lot of excellent charities out there who could really do with your help.

There are hundreds of charities involved in the Flora London Marathon and each year well over £30 million is raised for worthy causes. When deciding on the charity that you want to run for, you need to ask yourself a few questions. Have you any real affinity with the charity? Do you know much about it? Are there any personal or family reasons why you should run for it? How easy do you think it will be to run for that charity?

When trying to secure one of the guaranteed charity places, many runners will focus on one charity. This will be one that they have real, genuine reasons to support. The charity will often recognize this and offer a place as a result. From the charity's perspective this is a runner who is more likely to really get into their fundraising and hence to reach their target. Many other runners, however, try the multi-application approach. By applying to many charities at the same time you may increase your chances of getting a place, but it may not be one that you really want to run for. You could well find fundraising tough and your whole race experience could suffer as a result. Be targeted in who you talk to and think about the charity side of the arrangement. Be committed to the cause and everyone benefits.

Once you've had your place confirmed then your attention should turn to your new dual challenges – training and fundraising. If you got a charity place in an event then the fundraising is essential, but if you have a standard entry then it is optional.

Remember also that the charity will invest a lot of money in you over the next few months and if you pull out it could well cost them significant sums. Many people have to pull out each year through injury – some of these because training plans haven't been followed – but others pull out simply because they haven't done enough preparation and realize they will not be able to finish. The Flora London Marathon has two dates that are crucial. One is the date by which the organizers must receive the charity runners' entry forms and the other is when runner replacements must be submitted. If you withdraw after the second date and you have a guaranteed place from a charity that charity will not be able to replace you and they will receive no income from that place for that year's race. For any sized charity this can have a major impact, with potentially damaging effects on its work. Think carefully about withdrawing and remember the implications. If you are genuinely injured there is nothing anyone can do, but if it is for reasons that you could do something about then think carefully and if you have doubts then withdraw early and don't leave it until a date when the charity can no longer replace you.

Remember too that if you have a guaranteed place from a charity, rather than a place direct from the race organizer and you do pull out you may not be offered the place again by that charity. In many cases you will, but there are no guarantees. The place belongs to the charity and not the runner.

Running for charity can be a great experience as you can benefit from a comprehensive range of support services that could make all the difference to your race-day experience.

03

you're in, now what?

In this chapter you will learn:
- how to fit it all in
- how to make a diary of targets
- how to keep a training log.

Tip at the top
It is important to keep a training log and monitor your progress against a series of short-, medium- and long-term goals.

Getting a place in some marathons is not much of a challenge, but getting one in a race like the Flora London Marathon or the ING New York City Marathon is a completely different story. When you receive notification in the post from these two you feel a sense of achievement even before you've got anywhere near the start line, let alone the finish line!

Notification from the organizers of the Flora London Marathon comes in the form of a magazine known in the trade as the 'accepted' magazine; if you don't get in you receive a copy of the 'rejected' version. The ballot for places is heavily oversubscribed so if you receive an accepted copy you have done very well indeed. There are other ways of getting a place such as the charity route, but these places are also becoming more and more sought after.

So if you do get a place what should you do next? Most people's reaction is first and foremost to panic. Applying for a place in the Flora London Marathon is literally a lottery and if you do find out you have a place through the ballot then it can come as a bit of a shock! It's pretty easy to get in to most other marathons – you just enter online (in most cases) and you're in a few minutes later, unless entries have already closed (it should already have told you that on the website).

If you've got a place in the ballot you will find out during the first week of December and that gives you plenty of time to follow a comprehensive training plan that will get you to the start line in April in good shape – assuming you have done some running recently. If you are a complete beginner it is a good idea to undertake some basic training before you enter the race as four months isn't very long to train if you don't have much of a fitness history.

Whatever your background it is wise to visit your doctor to let him/her know what you're planning and have a check up. This is particularly important if you haven't exercised for some time. If you are carrying a few extra pounds you will be putting yourself under some pressure for the first few weeks so it's essential that you let a professional medical practitioner have a look at you.

After getting over the shock (or otherwise, depending on the event!) of getting a place and then having a medical check up, it is essential that you take stock and do some planning. There are some key things that you should do next.

Talk it through with friends and family

As we've discussed, running a marathon is a life-changing event and not just for yourself, but also those close to you. You must accept that it is going to impact on many people's lives and it is essential that you talk it through with them at the earliest opportunity. You will be spending many days and nights training and this time has got to come from somewhere. Most people now lead busy, hectic lives and it is likely that this time will have to be taken from time that you would normally be spending with those people closest to you. You and they all need to understand this at an early stage to avoid any misunderstanding or confusion later. You don't want an 'it's me or the marathon' type of confrontation in the middle of your training programme! You are going to need as much support as you can get when the training picks up, so take them with you throughout your journey – don't leave them behind!

Compile a training programme and stick with it

Be realistic when you select a plan, because once you're on it you don't want to change to another one after a few weeks. If you think that you're going to find it hard to commit as much time as you would like then select the 'get-you-round' plan. Be cautious when you're forecasting your potential finish time. Four hours might sound easy enough when you're sitting on the sofa thinking about running the event, but after a few weeks of training it may well seem a very distant dream. To run for four hours you need to be very committed to your training and be prepared to run five times a week for the last two months of your training at a pretty decent pace. It also means being able to run a half marathon in about one hour and forty-five minutes.

And a three-hour marathon ... that's a completely different story again!

Stick to your plan once you have selected it. It is definitely not a good idea to keep switching between plans, for a number of reasons. These include the amount of conditioning that each plan includes in the early stages. If you follow the 'get-you-round' plan it will include an amount of conditioning for the 'real running' that follows. If you then switch to the four-hour plan after a few weeks you will not have done the required level of conditioning for that plan and you may well become injured. Injuries are the curse of many people training for a marathon and in many cases it is because they have not trained correctly. They may have trained well, but just not in the correct way – in most cases without the right amount of conditioning, in other words a lack of the right sort of preparatory running.

Decide how you are going to fit it all in

Marathon training isn't the type of activity that you can just squeeze into an already full schedule; you will need to make some adjustments to your current way of life to make it all work.

Most of us do actually have the time to make it work – we might just not know it. Think about what TV programmes you can do without or how you can change your daily work schedule. Could you run before work, or during lunch? Getting home late often makes it difficult to run at night, but you will have to make changes so think carefully from the outset how you are going to fit it in.

This also goes for the long runs at the weekend and the events that will form an important part of your marathon build-up. If your weekends are full of another sport or pastime then you may need to put it on hold for a while. Once you are well into your training plan your long run will be anything between one and three hours, and when you add in the time it takes to get ready, stretch and then stretch and shower when you get back you are looking at around four to five hours towards the end of the plan. This will be one day at the weekend but the other day will also involve some training, so don't make too many plans outside of your running!

Make a diary of short-, medium- and long-term targets

Your marathon training consists of a number of key points, with the end game of actually completing the event being just one of them. There are a lot of important stages in between, including running your first five-kilometre event and then, in due course, a half marathon. You will need to put aside at least five Sundays for these events, from January through April if it's London you're running and the corresponding time period for other marathons.

As soon as you know you have a place in your marathon of choice you need to select the build-up events. Have a look at www.realbuzz.com for a comprehensive list of races of all distances and start planning as soon as possible in line with the training programme you have selected. It will tell you when you need to be running a race of a certain distance, so work out what week corresponds to what date and book them in. Most of these build-up races will be pretty easy to get into, apart from some of the big half marathons that are part of the Flora London Marathon build-up. You will need to get into these as soon as you can. Don't leave it until the last minute or you could be travelling much further than you need to for an event. You can enter most of them online.

It's important to get these events in your diary as soon as you can, as mentally it is good to have goals to aim for along the way. In the early stages you don't want to be worrying about the big 26.2 mile distance, you should be more concerned with running for three miles or five miles, ten miles and then a half marathon. These interim distances should be your real focus and being able to run in a properly organized race with hundreds of others all doing the same can be a real motivator. Many people lose heart during their training as all they can think about is the big picture and not the series of smaller ones along the way.

Keep a training log

Motivation is the key to your marathon training and one of the biggest motivators is to keep a training log. There are many different types available and you can make up your own using a notepad. One of the most fun to keep is a web log or 'blog' and on www.realbuzz.com you can choose from a number of different formats, including one for those running in London. Blogs allow you to maintain a diary of your progress online and also allow others to add comments. Those on realbuzz.com allow you to decide whether these posts from others are accepted and shown on your blog or not. It also includes a facility that sends emails to friends and family on your list of contacts every time you add a post to your blog. This enables you to keep loved ones up to date with your progress, which as we talked about above is particularly important.

The training log, whether it be an online blog, a specially written computer programme or a notepad serves a number of roles, each of them very important. We'll cover these in more detail in the training section. Don't leave it too long before you set up your training log, the sooner you start the better. It's great to see the entries accumulating as you run and you don't want to miss any run, however small, off the list!

Start thinking about your kit

There is a separate chapter on choosing the right gear, but one of the most important aspects of making these choices is to do it quickly and with professional advice. If you are an absolute beginner, or even a runner who goes out every now and again, chances are that you may not have the right gear. You do not want to begin your marathon training with incorrect kit, especially your running shoes, so get down to your local running specialist as soon as you can. Have your feet measured properly by someone with experience and take advice on what brand and model of shoe to buy – more on this later.

If you have received news on your Flora London Marathon place then chances are this will have been in December so no guesses on what your Christmas wish list should consist of. Make sure you give people a helping hand though and suggest some products that you've already tried on, or which have been recommended as essential.

Enjoy it!

Finally, if you have managed to secure a sought-after place in one of the big events then think how lucky you are and enjoy the whole process from the day you find out you have a place to the day you cross the finish line – you are one of the lucky ones.

If you are running one of the other marathons for which getting a place isn't so difficult then you will also be about to embark on the journey of a lifetime, enjoy it!

04

the right gear

In this chapter you will learn:
- about the benefits of the right gear
- what to wear and when
- how to choose running shoes
- what accessories you need.

We've all seen them. You're in the car and suddenly out of nowhere appears what looks like a cross between the abominable snowman and an entrant in the local fancy dress competition. This is the poorly prepared runner, the runner who hasn't found the world of wicking and breathable fabrics. This is the throwback to the 1970s, someone who has missed out on the technical revolution.

Today's runner is confronted with a series of technical developments that has transformed the sport in a surprisingly short time. There is now absolutely no excuse for getting it wrong. Walk into a modern running shop and you will be overwhelmed by the choice of gear that you can choose from. Some of it you can do without and much of it you can't, but most important of all you need to understand it. You must find out what's what and make some informed decisions about what you really need.

Running isn't a particularly expensive hobby compared with many, but you must be aware that you will have to invest if you are to get the most from it. Be prepared to spend around £200 to £250 to get started and remember that it won't stop there. You will need to regularly replace kit as your training progresses. At least you don't have the initial outlay associated with some sports. Imagine if you were beginning your triathlon training and you had to choose a bike!

The benefits of wearing the right gear

There are a number of reasons why you should make sure that you get the right gear from day one.

It will help you run better

Wearing the right gear will make a fundamental difference to the way that you run. Many runners overheat even after a few miles, especially in the cold weather when they wear too much and often the wrong type of clothing. Many wear clothes that chafe, rub or cut badly. Poor-fitting clothing or the wrong type of clothing often leads to poor performance, which in turn leads to a reduction in morale. It is hard enough to keep your motivation levels high, especially in the middle of winter, so the last thing you need is to make it even more difficult by wearing the wrong gear.

The more lightweight your gear is the better. You need to keep your extra weight down to a minimum. Kit these days is extremely light; in fact it is much lighter than it has ever been before so make the most of the options available. The heavier the gear the harder it is to get round. Buy well and it will make a real difference to your running.

It will help prevent injury

There will be many ways to pick up injuries during your training so it essential to do everything in your power to prevent them. One way is to wear the correct clothing and footwear. Get this wrong and you will be well on your way to trouble.

One of the principal reasons why so many runners get injured is because of problems with their shoes. If they are too small you can have problems, if they are too big you can have problems and if they are the wrong type you can have problems! As you can see, the potential for problems is enormous.

Even the wrong clothing can cause injuries, although not to the same degree as incorrect footwear and they may not be as serious. Tight-fitting gear can cause rubbing and chaffing which can get so bad that it can prevent you training. It may even lead to infections if you aren't careful. Loose-fitting clothing can also rub, so whatever you do make sure that you buy gear that fits.

Safety first

Wearing the right gear can also save your life. It is very likely that training for a northern hemisphere spring marathon like the Flora London Marathon will mean training in the dark and this can, by definition, be a dangerous occupation, especially if you are forced to run on roads with no pavements. It is therefore essential that you wear kit that includes reflective strips, which many high-tech fabrics now do, or that you wear a stand-alone reflective band that you can buy in most decent running shops. Wear old gear and chances are it doesn't include any reflective qualities.

Makes you feel good

Wearing the latest gear isn't just about looking good, or being safe and injury free, it is also about feeling good. There is no doubt that for most runners the happier you feel about the way you look, the more confident you will be and ultimately the better you will run. Don't assume, however, that better-dressed runners automatically run better. That definitely isn't the case. There is no doubt though that the happier you are with yourself the more you will enjoy your running and, as a result, the more likely you are to improve your performance.

This doesn't mean you have to keep changing your tops each month just to keep the fashion police happy, it just means wearing the right fabrics and keeping up with technical changes.

Running through the seasons

As your training progresses so you will be exposed to the joys of running through the seasons. If you are training for the Flora London Marathon in April you will have the toughest conditions, whereas if it's New York you've chosen then you'll have the best of them as you'll be training over the summer. There are, of course, pros and cons to running at either time of year, and very different kit requirements.

Warm-weather training

Between May and September your running wardrobe will be fundamentally different from the one that you will be familiar with in the colder months. In late spring and during the summer you will have to wear very little, with a pair of running shorts, T-shirt or vest being the principal items of clothing.

It is, however, important to ensure that you prepare well for your runs. You should wear a hat to protect your head from the sun and also you should invest in a quality pair of sunglasses. Sun cream is also vital. A long run in sunny conditions will expose much of your body to damaging rays and you must protect yourself accordingly. Avoid running in the heat of the day if you can, especially at midday. Early morning and late evening are the best options, but whenever you go make sure that you take some water to keep yourself well hydrated.

Thin socks are a must if it is hot as they will go some way to keeping your feet cool. In especially warm climates running shoes are adapted to take the heat into account. They will often use more mesh, for example, than is used in regions like the UK.

With whatever you wear the key is to keep layers light and protect yourself thoroughly from the sun.

Cold-weather training

Layers are also the key in cold-weather training but for a different reason. Many runners, particularly those starting out on their running career, tend to react to the cold by wearing the thickest tops they can find as protection from the elements. This is fundamentally wrong.

The way to protect yourself from the cold is to wear layers, which trap air between them that acts as insulation. As you warm up you can then remove layers if needed to keep your body temperature at the optimum level. These layers, which should also be of the correct fabrics, will help disperse the sweat that builds up during your training. The opposite applies if you wear thick clothing of the wrong fabrics. Sweat will build up, and it is not advisable to remove clothing if you are only wearing one or two thick items, as your temperature will plummet.

Avoid fleeces and thick cotton shirts and if you are planning to wear a rain jacket make sure that is made of a breathable fabric.

Invest in a good pair of running gloves, a hat and leggings, again all made from breathable fabric.

Shoes

Walk into a big running shop, look at the running shoe selection and it is likely that you will be instantly confused. There is a huge variety of products on the market and many of them will never be of any relevance to you at all. There are not only many different brands available with many different models from each brand, but there are also different shoes for men and women and then different types based on which category you fit into.

The world of running shoes is a world full of marketing jargon. You will be bombarded with 'technical' benefits that are generally the same in most shoes but with a slightly different name depending on the brand. Shoes have improved dramatically in the last few years with changes, particularly in cushioning, that help reduce the incidence of injuries. A small number of brands dominate the market but just because you haven't heard of a certain brand doesn't mean you should write it off before you've tried it on. Many of the smaller running shoe brands only operate within this sector, have small marketing budgets but sell most of their product based on recommendations from other runners. They may only have a small share of the marketplace but this does not imply a lack of quality but more likely a lack of marketing spend.

It is important when selecting your first pair of shoes that you make the effort and find a specialist running store. Most good-sized towns have one, but if yours hasn't then it is well worth travelling to one that has. You must have specialist advice because if you get it wrong then you could well have a running career blighted by injury and discomfort ahead. This is your most important purchase and you must make a choice based on facts that you have researched yourself and that you have been given at the point of purchase. Head to a high-street sports retailer on a Saturday afternoon in December and it is very likely that you will come away with the wrong shoes. Try a specialist retailer and it is very likely that you will get it right. Most specialist outlets are staffed by runners and that will make a major difference. Another advantage of visiting a specialist retailer is that they very often have treadmills. The reason for this is to enable the staff to watch you run for a few minutes so they can check your running style or 'gait'. This will be analysed on a computer screen and from the information provided decisions can be made on the best shoes for you. Not all running stores have these (some will rely on a visual test, in other words watching you run inside or outside the shop), but it is definitely a good idea to find one that does.

There are a number of different price points, with shoes starting at around £50 and going up to around £120. The highest does not always mean the best, although more often than not you get what you pay for, as with anything in life. If you have set a budget, try and be flexible if the best-fitting and most comfortable shoe of the three that you've tried on is a little more expensive than you were planning on spending. This purchase is a crucial one and comfort is the key. As, of course, is injury prevention. Invest and you will enjoy your running much more.

Socks

Most beginners would assume a sock is a sock. A pack of three white cotton socks is generally seen to be sufficient to get you through many months of training. As with most sports, however, all is not what it seems. There is now almost as great a choice of running socks as there is shoes, with many brands offering technology that is a world away from the situation as recently as five years ago.

Choose carefully and you can potentially reduce the development of blisters, ease pressure on your Achilles tendon and look after your instep. Now it's not all about a multi-pack of cotton socks, it is about investing wisely and getting advice on what is right for you before you buy.

Go through the door of any decent running shop and you will be amazed by the choice of running socks from at least six brand names. Each of them will have seemingly endless options, giving you a huge headache – which ones do you really need? Speak to one of the staff and get help, just as you would when choosing a pair of running shoes. Get the wrong one and you could be in trouble, but the get the right one and your running could become much easier on your feet.

One of the most significant changes in recent years is the introduction of blister-resistant technology. Although there are of course no guarantees, the use of two layers of fabric has made the world of difference to many runners prone to persistent blisters. The two layers of fabric rub against each other rather than your foot, easing friction, one of the causes of blisters; at the same time they draw away moisture, one of the other causes. Try a pair and see how you get on. It is well worth paying the extra!

Many sock manufacturers also produce socks anatomically designed for each of your feet. They are subtlety different and again are worth a try. Each is easily identified by a distinctive 'L' and 'R'.

Whatever you do, do not just buy a multi-pack of basic cotton socks and think that this is your feet looked after. It is not and you must spend time getting your footwear right. That means your shoes and socks.

Underwear

There are a number of companies marketing sports underwear, but if you're not ready to invest in it yet don't worry, you don't really have to. The key point, however, is to keep your underwear brief. You shouldn't be wearing thick, heavy underwear and it shouldn't be too baggy. Boxer shorts, for example, aren't the best idea for men. Keep it brief and snug but not too tight.

Sports bras

Sports bras are an industry in their own right, with some retailers both on and offline selling virtually nothing else! All women should consider wearing one, whatever your size, and when you make your choice don't just go for the first one that you find.

You must not assume that one bra will do the job for an indefinite amount of time. Generally you should look to get a replacement after about four months of moderate use. You should monitor how well it supports your bust, with increased movement or rubbing indicating that a change is needed.

Getting the right size from the start is crucial. Your bra should never be too tight and if there is any bulging then it is not the right fit. Ideally you should be able to place two fingers under the band. Take your time getting it right and ideally visit a retailer who has experience in this area. Choosing the right size and the right make for you will ensure that your running is a lot more comfortable!

Shorts

If you have ever tried on a pair of running shorts you have probably already made the decision that this is not the type of gear that you want to be seen in. They are, to put it mildly, brief and in many cases men's underwear is more substantial. They are designed with one thing in mind and that is speed. They are, of course, extremely lightweight and high cut, which means you hardly feel like you are wearing them. If you are looking to take seconds off your best time they are the way forward but if you are just starting out then you should look at other options.

These other options are many and varied. You can choose whatever length shorts you prefer, which will differ significantly depending on what you are prepared to be seen in. Don't wear anything that is too long as it can be uncomfortable and can lead to chaffing. Look also for shorts with internal and external pockets where you can keep cash, keys and other essentials. For men, shorts with an internal 'brief' stitched inside are also worth looking at as they avoid the need to wear underpants and can also double up as swimming trunks.

Tight cycling shorts are worn by many runners. They are often recommended by physios as a form of injury prevention, especially for groin problems.

Whatever style suits you, make sure that comfort is at the top of your list of priorities. Don't go for something too big or too small and bear in mind that your size may reduce as your running career develops.

Leggings

Running on cold winter nights means running in leggings. These aren't always the most flattering garment in your running wardrobe but they play a vital role as the temperature plummets. Not only will they actually keep you warm but they will assist with injury prevention by keeping your leg muscles warm. Cold weather is often when muscles get pulled and the warmer you can keep them, without overheating of course, the better.

There are many different types of leggings on the market as you would expect, and again you need to make the right choice for you. You will wear them a great deal between November and February and if you get the wrong pair you will dread the cold nights. Try on a few options at your nearest specialist running store and ask about the fabric that each is made from. Breathable fabric is used in many and that is an especially important factor that you should take into account. Don't assume an old pair of tracksuit trousers will do the job: they won't. You must go for something designed for the job, if you are too keep warm and allow the sweat to 'wick' away from your body as it should.

Most leggings come in black, but more and more colour options are becoming available.

Tops

Seeing red-faced runners is very common and more often than not it is a result of wearing tops made of the wrong materials. It is essential that you do not run in cotton tops or any other material that is non-wicking. Wicking is the process in which sweat is drawn away from the skin and evaporates away. If this does not take place the moisture will remain on your body and when it gets cold will cause you significant discomfort. Add a cold Siberian wind and life can get very nasty!

Rugby tops and fleeces are very popular and again are probably the worst tops that you can wear. They are far too heavy and there is absolutely no wicking quality at all. They will cause you nothing but problems and should be avoided at all costs.

Stick with the principle of layering and wear quality tops that you can buy from any decent running shop. It is far more advisable to wear two tops designed for the purpose than one thick one that is not. Layering traps air and gives you significant insulation, a process that does not take place with the thick, single-layer approach.

Jackets

The same principle applies to jackets as to tops. Keep them light and make sure that the one you select is made from the correct wicking fabric. The heavier your jacket the more difficult you will find it to run. It will feel far too bulky and could well affect your running technique. You will almost certainly overheat and if the jacket does not wick sweat it will become heavier as the run progresses. Add the rain which will be absorbed rather than deflected and you could be in for a hard time.

Ideally you need a very light jacket which acts as a windbreak and which lets your skin breathe correctly. It should be a jacket that you hardly know you're wearing, and if it isn't uncomfortable at the start of your run then it certainly will be by the finish.

Make sure that it also has reflective strips to help keep you well seen.

Gloves

As with all running gear, there are numerous different types of running gloves available and the technology has moved on a great deal in recent years. Fabrics have been revolutionised and modern running gloves now keep your hands very warm without them sweating. They are very light and often come in bright fluorescent colours to help you be seen in the dark. Even the black ones often include reflective strips.

There may be some days in deepest winter when you might feel the lightweight gloves aren't enough. If that is case then try a pair of ski gloves which will most definitely do the job. This should, however, be the exception rather than the rule as the wicking qualities of this type of glove are somewhat limited.

Hats

Never underestimate the importance of a hat! Heat escapes through your head and on cold winter runs in the middle of February you will need every bit of heat you can find. Equally, a hat will protect you from the sun on your warmer runs.

Again, there are plenty of options, with plenty of different fabrics. In the winter it's best to consider a thick hat that will give you plenty of insulation. Made with specialist fabrics they will allow sweat to evaporate and will keep your head cool while still retaining heat. Try a hat made from non-specialist fibre and you may not find that to be the case.

In the summer go for a lightweight baseball cap. It is important that you protect yourself from the sun and feel comfortable at the same time. Too much weight on your head on a hot day is not the way forward!

Sunglasses

This is a piece of kit where there really is the most incredible level of choice. Whatever type, style and colour of product you are looking for you will find it. The options are limitless. You must, however, put style to one side and consider a number of important points.

It might sound obvious, but check that the glasses you are considering contain the correct safety glass. They don't always, so be careful and don't just go for the style or the colour. If they aren't safe then don't even think about buying them.

Make sure they are comfortable. Again that might sound incredibly obvious but it is very common for style to be the key factor for many runners. You are going to be covering many miles in your sunglasses and they must feel good if you are to enjoy wearing them. Jog on the spot for a few minutes when you're trying them on, don't be content with a look in the mirror. Many glasses will feel fine when you're standing still but not when you're moving!

Think about ventilation. Some are better than others in this area and it is important that you ask for advice on this aspect of your sunglasses before making the purchase.

Watches and other accessories

Every month is seems that the world of timing becomes even more sophisticated. You can now spend hundreds of pounds of products that will do almost anything, from the most basic function to the most complex. If your budget is tiny you will find something to suit your needs and if you have plenty to spend then the options are endless.

Running watches

Running watches come in all shapes and sizes and can be as multi-functioned as you like. For most beginners all you really need is one with a stop watch and a light. You need to know how long you have been running for and that is pretty much it. Then you can move on to lap times if you use a running track or loop of a park, for example. The next stage is a heart-rate function which helps you work out how hard you are training.

Heart-rate monitors

After your initial introduction to running you may well want to invest in a heart-rate monitor to help you work out how effectively you are training. Training in the correct 'zone' is very important and a heart-rate monitor will let you know if you are getting it right. Most HRMs also include a watch, stopwatch and backlight so it makes sense to go for a basic model straight away, rather than a watch to begin with and then monitor later. You don't have to pay much more than £30 to £40 to get a product that will do the job, but if you think you might want more, like a downloadable facility to your PC, you are looking at over £100. These products have features you may never need but for those that like gadgets they are perfect!

Speed and distance monitors

Gadgets don't come much better than speed and distance monitors. Often with a timing and heart-rate monitor inbuilt they allow you to measure exactly how far you are running and at what speed per mile or kilometre. They come in all shapes and sizes with part of the device either worn on the arm or a shoe, and they work using global positioning systems. GPS receivers pick up signals sent from satellites and use the information to pinpoint exactly where you are. Add the relevant software and you have a speed and distance monitor.

These monitors are invaluable as you increase your training and as your aspirations change. You can gauge exactly how well your training is going and plan new routes with ease. Mapping software enables you to develop new runs and find out exactly how far they are beforehand, without the need to get in the car and test them out.

Pedometers

Another way of measuring distance is the use of a pedometer. Some are more accurate than others, and as with most things, you get what you pay for. Invest £5 and you won't be able to guarantee exactly how far you've run, but spend £30 and the reliability improves significantly. These gadgets are generally all about calibration and the more time you spend setting them up correctly the more you can then trust the results. If you really want accuracy go for a speed and distance monitor, but if you want more of a guide pedometers are much, much cheaper.

Hydration and nutrition accessories

There will be many occasions when you are on a run and you need water or some food and you have none with you. This is when belts and water bottles come into their own.

It is not a good idea to carry water bottles in your hand as they can adversely affect your posture. Some are ergonomically shaped with a hand grip, but even these when full can alter the way that you run and can cause long-term problems like shoulder pain. This is a very common pain for runners who carry bottles in this way. The unnatural running style creates stress which manifests itself in shoulder problems that are easily rectified by a more relaxed, bottle-free approach.

The alternative is a specially designed belt into which you can slot bottles, gels, chocolate bars, energy drinks and pretty much anything that you think will make your run more enjoyable! On a long run, just prior to your first marathon, you may well need one of these belts as leaving water at strategic locations along the route could be difficult.

Music

Running with music has never been as popular as it is now. This is primarily a result of the growth of the mp3 player, especially the iPod. These devices are not only lightweight but for the first time you can now run without your favourite track skipping a beat at regular intervals! Listening to music on the move has never been as easy as it is now thanks to some major advances in technology. The days of carrying portable CD players have gone and limitless song choice has arrived.

There is no doubt that running with music can make a difference, particularly on repetitive routes, but it is not to everyone's taste. It is definitely not a good idea at big city-centre events like New York or London as the noise from the crowd and other runners is one of the most enjoyable aspects of the days. To that end it is important not to run with music every day so you can at least get used to running without it in preparation for the big day.

If you do find inspiration from music, the mp3 player has changed the market completely and is the only real option.

05 training

In this chapter you will learn:
- how to get started
- the right technique
- the principles of training
- how to stretch.

Tip at the top
Rest is an important aspect of your training – be sensible and enjoy your time off, you will have deserved it!

One of the most important elements of your preparation for your first marathon is to allow yourself plenty of time to train. Those who fail to get to the start line often do so because they just did not give themselves enough time to prepare. This is one of the biggest physical challenges of your life and you must allow your body enough time to adapt to the many changes that it will go through.

Most first timers wonder how it will be possible. How can I go from being able to run for a few minutes to running for five hours or so in a marathon (potentially much longer for some beginners)? It can be done, but it takes time and it is time that many people simply run out of.

Ideally you need to allow yourself at least six months for your training programme, depending on your level of fitness. If you really are an absolute beginner another couple of months are preferable and likewise, if you are running a couple of times a week already then you can do it in a few weeks less. It is all about conditioning your body to something it is not used to and ensuring that injuries are minimized. The more running you currently do the less time is needed to prepare.

If you try and cut corners it is very likely that your body will complain and injuries will occur. These are generally a reaction to the stress that you are placing your body under, and the tighter the timescales the more stress. Prepare correctly over many months and the chances of injury are reduced.

You also need to factor in the likelihood of coming down with a cold or flu virus, which is very common, especially over the cold winter months that are the basis of your Flora London Marathon training programme. A couple of weeks missed at this stage could seriously damage your chances if you have a tight programme. If you have plenty of time to train then it will be much less of a concern.

Leave yourself plenty of time and you will find the whole process much more enjoyable.

Before you start

Running a marathon is an extreme personal challenge and the training can push your body to its limit before you even get on the start line. When you have finished the training you will be a changed person, but then for the real challenge – getting round 26.2 miles!

You must take this whole process very seriously and understand the demands that you will be placing on both your body and mind. Before you do anything you must see your doctor, discuss your plans and get the all clear to start the programme. There is a huge variety in fitness levels of those beginning their training, with some having plenty of running experience and some having absolutely none. Don't risk your health – get yourself checked out.

Some of the questions you are likely to be asked are:

- Are you 30 or over and/or have not exercised for a while?
- Have you any medical history?
- Are you a smoker or have you recently quit?
- Are you on medication?
- Have you any history of injury?
- Have you any concerns about the challenge ahead?

Answer honestly!

How do you start?

There is a very simple answer to this question and it is 'slowly'. One of the most common mistakes made by first-time marathon runners is to run as far as they can on their first run. They run until they can't run any more and are so disillusioned by how bad they feel that they never run again. This is completely the wrong approach. You should run/walk for the prescribed time and always feel like you have a bit left, in other words, stop your session thinking that you could actually have gone a little bit further. Many runners who succumb to a premature end to their marathon aspirations simply do too much too soon.

If you are totally new to the running game then it is very important that your first training sessions aren't running at all. They could be walking sessions or introductory days in the gym where you build up your heart and lung capabilities. You should not begin running until you have built up some stamina and worked on leg strengthening. The latter can be achieved by a good walking schedule over a few weeks. You must give your legs some preparation before suddenly putting them through months of running.

If you are already running on a reasonably regular basis again it is all about slow progression. If the most you have ever run is twenty minutes then your next session should be 21 minutes, not 31.

Technique

There are numerous running styles, many of which you can observe on a regular basis. While it is easy to adopt your own style, which you will feel is the right one and the most natural for you, there is very much a right way and a wrong way to run.

The key components of a fluid and economical running style are described below.

Heel to toe foot movement

You should never bring your foot flat down, but instead hit the ground with your heel first and then your toes. This will allow you to 'spring' into the next step. You should almost bounce from one step to the next, which will obviously prove more challenging the further you run!

Head still and looking ahead, not down

As you run you should be looking ahead and keeping your head still. Resist the temptation to look down at the floor for the duration of your run. Obviously you will need to check where you are running periodically but don't do it all the time.

Regular deep breathing

Many runners pay little or no attention to their breathing and run poorly as a result, especially towards the end of a run. It is important not to keep exhaling but breathe in deeply on a regular basis. Every hundred metres or so you should drop the arms and breathe in deeply through the nose. Exhale slowly through the mouth – this should take twice as long as the breath in – and then bring the arms back to the correct position. This will open up the heart and lungs, so improving their functionality and increase the amount of oxygen in your body.

This is also the best way to avoid stitch or to sort it out if you do get it. Many runners assume stitch strikes as a result of eating too close to a run and that is very often the case, but it also regularly hits runners who are not breathing correctly.

Arms should be low and swinging

One of the common mistakes with runners of all levels is the position of the arms. Ideally the arms should be down by your sides, bent at the elbow and lightly brushing your waist as you run. They should not be drawn across your chest and they should not be too high. There are three primary reasons for this.

First, the higher that you carry your arms the more pain you will get in your shoulders. Shoulder and upper back pain is extremely common in runners of all levels and in the majority of cases it is because of incorrect technique. Keep your arms low and you will ease the pressure on your shoulders as you are not putting them under duress. If you have your arms high your shoulders are in effect 'holding them up' and using up valuable energy.

Second, by keeping your arms away from your chest the more open your heart and lungs are and the more efficiently they can function. By bringing your arms across your body you constrict your cardiovascular system, making it more difficult for it to work to its maximum potential.

Third, by allowing free movement of your arms by your sides they can operate more effectively like car pistons and drive you forward. If you have maximum movement, you can use your arms to their full potential. This is especially evident up hills where the more you can drive with your arms the more effective and economical your running performance.

Run in an upright position and don't slouch

Never run in a bolt upright position but at the same time ensure that you do not slouch. As your run progresses, particularly a long run, you will notice that you almost start to lean forward. You must avoid this and keep your posture intact. Don't run 100 per cent upright, but instead aim for about 90 per cent. By looking ahead and keeping your head still this is the position that you should naturally adopt.

Don't carry anything in your hands

Avoid the temptation to carry water bottles, music, gels or anything else! You can easily wear a belt to which you can add anything you think you'll need on your run and this will avoid the need for running with anything in your hand. Running with a heavy water bottle is one of the most common reasons for poor running technique. The hand that is carrying the bottle will put a lot more stress on the shoulder and can easily lead to significant pain as a result. More often than not it will lead to an uneven running style with one arm much higher than the other. This leads to an inefficient cardiovascular system and poor breathing technique.

Training principles

Before embarking on a training programme it is important to understand the four rules of training. These rules are known as 'the principles of training'.

Progression

Endurance running is all about gradual progression. It is all about slowly adding more time each week and never pushing yourself to a point where you feel totally uncomfortable. As you progress your body should feel the difference, but it should never be to the point where you are not capable of going a little bit further.

Ideally each week you should add around five to ten per cent more time to your training. By using 'time on feet' rather than mileage, you can slowly build up how much you run. Over time you will get quicker and you will run more distance in each session, but at the start you should focus on how long you are actually out of the house for, not how far you go.

Progression is the absolute cornerstone of your training and why you must allow yourself plenty of time. Rush your training and you may well become succumb to the runners' worst nightmare – the injury curse. Take it nice and steady and you will allow your legs to strengthen and your heart and lungs to become efficient, so allowing them to cope with the challenge that they face.

Specificity

While the principle of cross training is important it is vital to remember that you must focus your training on the discipline you have chosen. In other words, if you have decided to run a marathon you must spend the majority of your time running and not swimming, cycling or on other cardiovascular activities. This is because you must put stress on the parts of your body that you will use in the event itself. Don't develop muscles that you aren't going to use and focus on those you will be using!

Individualization

Everyone is different and everyone will respond to a training programme in a different way. While it is always good to train with others you may not always find it easy. Two complete beginners starting out together may not develop at the same rate and will often respond at different times to different elements of their schedule. You will regularly have off days, but they may not be the same days as your training partner even though you are following exactly the same plan and starting from the same level of fitness. Some people simply respond better than others.

Overload

Often confused with overtraining, which is when you train too much without enough rest, overload is an important part of a planned schedule. Overload is an increased exposure to an increased workload followed by the correct level of rest. The weekend long run is overload and is without doubt the most critical element of your marathon training programme. Overtraining would result if you did not build in the right amount of rest and kept training too hard without breaks.

The long run

Your weekly training programme will consist of anything from three to six sessions, depending on your level of fitness. The fitter you get the more sessions you will be able to add to your programme and the more you will be able to cope. During the week your sessions will be fairly similar, although as the weeks progress so too will the amount of time you spend on your feet in each session. It is at the weekend, though, when you will notice the biggest change. The weekend is the home of the long run and it is this which is the most important part of your running training.

The long run is the real test of how well your training is going. Too many runners keep their training distances constant all week and never push on to a longer distance, which is absolutely essential if you are to prepare yourself for the marathon properly. This comes back to the training principle of overload. You must push yourself a bit further on one occasion each week and then give yourself the chance to recover with the appropriate rest period. The long run is not something that you will necessarily look forward to but it is crucial to your success on race day and if you don't run far enough in training you will struggle when it comes to your big moment! The nearer you get to marathon day the more you will become fixated by the long run. During the week you prepare and then on Saturday or Sunday you go for it. Can you do two hours, two and a half, three or four?

Ideally you should run at least 20 miles before the marathon at least two weeks before the marathon and preferably three weeks beforehand. This will give you plenty of time to rest and to re-energize before race day. It will also give you a huge amount of confidence. This confidence is a vital part of your marathon armoury and will stand you in good stead as you get into the second half of the event. If you can run 20 miles or the equivalent percentage of time (if you are expecting to run five hours then you should run up to four hours) then rest assured that the crowd will get you through the rest of it. You do not need to run a full marathon in training. It is important that you really do take this on board from day one. All your long run training should be based on a maximum run of around 20 miles, not 26.2.

Tapering

Ten days or so before your marathon you will enter what is known as the taper period. The exact number of days depends on how well you listen to your body. If you listen well you will make sure that it is at least ten days, if you don't then it may well only be five or even less. This is the time when you must cut the running right back, eat well, relax and look forward to the fun ahead! It is this time when your race day can be made or destroyed.

Many novice runners are still training hard up until race day and many try and make up for time lost due to injuries or a cold. However, you must apply the taper period whether you have been able to follow a full schedule or if you have lost a month through a bad knee. You must be rested and refreshed when you stand on the start line irrespective of what has taken place in the preceding months.

It can be a very frustrating time for many. You are feeling at the peak of your running career and suddenly you have to cut back, even though you may not want to. You must not listen to the voices in your head that encourage you to do one last really long run in race week. Ignore the voices and cut it back. Your runs at this time should be 30 to 40 minutes on average and may just be brisk walks to keep your muscles warm. Listen to your body and give it a break. It will be put under serious stress on race day and you must allow it to prepare.

This period gives you a chance to prepare mentally and also to carry out kit checks and other logistical tasks that you may have neglected. Any last minute fundraising? Do it now!

The importance of rest

Rest is often looked on in a negative way by many runners, especially those who become a little bit obsessed as their training progresses. Rest is good and let no-one tell you different. Too much rest of course is not, and as with all things in life finding the balance is the key to marathon success. At the start of your programme you will have more rest days, but as your body adapts to the stress that you put it under these are reduced. You will find that your recovery times improve and you will not be as tired.

As a beginner it is very likely that you will feel extremely tired, especially after your weekend long runs and you will feel like constantly sleeping. As you become more experienced a run will make you feel invigorated rather than tired, but it takes a long time to get to that point. If you do not rest properly you will fall victim to overtraining and your running performance will be affected. You will feel overtired at work, become irritable with everyone and rapidly lose the support of those around you. This latter point is crucial. Lose support of your loved ones and you have a problem. You must keep them on side and resting properly will help you to do that.

This is again why you must leave yourself many months to train for your first marathon. You must give yourself every opportunity to rest and if you feel that you are running out of days you may well end up compromising on your time off. You must fight this. As touched on previously, resting sufficiently after the long run – the overload – is especially important. If you try running again too quickly you could at best be too tired, or at worst get a bad injury. Be sensible and enjoy your time off, you will have deserved it!

Different types of training

Training isn't just about pounding the streets day after day at the same pace. There are other options, although it is important to stress that these are more relevant as your training develops. In the first instance you should try and gradually increase the time you spend on your feet, ideally on flat routes. When you are up to the right stage in your training you can start to mix it up. You will know when you have reached that point and if you follow a training plan, as you should, then you will be advised when to make the change.

Hill training

Most of the world's leading marathons like London, Berlin and Chicago are run on virtually flat courses, while others like New York and Boston have one or two hills but are still predominantly flat. Hill training might seem an odd addition to your training, but there is a reason for it. Hills can build leg strength and aid in the development of your cardiovascular system that can't be achieved in the same timescales on the flat. There are many approaches to hill training, with some runners simply selecting routes with a certain number of hills, while others train using one or two key hills and run up and down a number of times or for a number of minutes. This can be extreme, but can have major physiological benefits. It is not something for beginners but, when you are looking to improve your times it is an option. Many of you will have no choice when it comes to hills – you have to run them. This is not necessarily bad for beginners, but you should try and keep on the flat as much as possible, with hillier routes added as you gain strength.

Fartlek training

The term 'fartlek' has taken on legendary status in the running world. It is actually Swedish for 'speed play', which in itself can still be confusing. It is again a type of training more for runners looking to improve their times than those more interested in just getting round their first marathon and where their time is not especially important. Speed play is the use of markers on your route for bursts of quicker running. For example, you may run past a line of trees or lamp posts and you alternate your speed between them – fast between one set of two, a slow recovery jog between the next two and then fast again between the next two.

This technique can have major benefits in developing heart and lungs, but it can also have a major downside if not managed correctly. Many beginners pick up injuries when attempting fartlek training and if you are thinking about it then take some advice from someone experienced in this approach.

The same goes for interval training.

Interval training

Interval training is again of more interest to marathon runners looking to trim a few minutes off their best time than those just looking to complete their first event.

It involves repetitions that are timed, often involving a running track. Runners will complete track circuits, or part circuits, in a certain time, have a break and then do the same again. Over time you will notice improvements in the time taken to complete the reps and also in the recovery period in between these reps.

All the elite athletes will incorporate a significant amount of interval training within their programme, but it will be very well supervised. Do not try serious intervals without some support, and stick to an agreed schedule.

Cross training

In the training principles outlined earlier in this chapter the concept of specificity was covered. This is the need to focus your training efforts on running in order to develop your body in the best way to deal with the marathon. If you have four sessions a week to train you would not spend three of them swimming, another one cycling and then expect to turn up on race day and finish the marathon comfortably.

However, there is a need to bring an element of cross training into your programme, albeit on a limited scale. Cross training can relieve pressure on your legs as you get deep into your training, so helping to prevent injury, and importantly it can help to ease boredom.

There will come a point in your programme when you really do feel like a break from running. While you should keep this break to a minimum you can substitute a running session for some cross training and you will not lose your fitness. Don't decide that you want a fortnight off and think that cycling will be a good alternative because it won't. It may keep you fit but it will not keep up your running fitness. Cross training is great way of staying fresh mentally and giving your legs a break, but not more than one session a week.

The best forms of cross training for runners are cycling, swimming and cardiovascular workout machines in the gym, like the rowing machine. Give your heart and lungs a really good workout and you will feel invigorated – ready for your next run!

Resistance training

This type of training is based around the lifting of weights in the gym, either free weights or using fixed machines. It is not core for beginners as most training time should be focused on building the endurance base needed for the challenge ahead, but if you do want one session a week in the gym and you have time for it then resistance training could be for you. Ask your gym instructor to devise a programme for you, taking into account your running programme and the work you will already be doing on your legs. This form of training will give you an all-over body workout and will work muscles that running can never touch. It will also help your core stability, important in injury prevention.

Warming up and cooling down

Before you begin your main session you should spend a few minutes warming up. This can be a brisk walk or a very light jog before you really get going. It serves to raise the heart rate and get the blood flowing to the muscles that really need it. Warming up is all about preparing yourself for the exercise that is to come.

It is then sensible to do some mobility work. This involves some light stretching to loosen up the joints and to make sure that they are fully lubricated.

When you have completed your main session it is important that you do not just stop, have a shower and get changed. You must cool down slowly and bring your heart rate back to near normal levels before even thinking about a shower. During exercise you generate a lot of waste by-products and these will be removed from your system much more effectively if you cool down in the right way. No cool down means a more prolonged recovery period thanks to the waste by-products still in the body.

Once you have cooled down then it's on to one of the most regularly forgotten elements of your session, flexibility work, more commonly known as stretching.

Stretching

Ask any runner if they should stretch and they will say yes. Ask if they actually do and the answer will invariably be something along the lines of 'sometimes, but not often enough'.

The main reason for this is that at the end of a run most runners just want to stop, have a shower and get dressed. Spending time cooling down and stretching just doesn't appeal. This is especially the case on a cold winter's night when the idea of a warm shower is particularly attractive.

But just why should you stretch – and how?

Stretching can play a major role in helping prevent injuries, it can improve your mobility and significantly affect your range and efficiency of movement, but if you get it wrong it can be potentially damaging. There is very much a wrong and a right way of doing it.

You should never stretch when you are cold. You must have warmed up, ensuring there is sufficient blood flow to the muscles. If you don't then there is a real chance of injury. You should also be relaxed. Tense muscles will reduce the effectiveness of the stretch. Take it easy when you stretch and ease in and out of each. Don't make sudden movements and do not bounce when you stretch, a common mistake particularly with inexperienced runners. After a few seconds, take the stretch a little bit further, making sure that you maintain your normal breathing pattern at all times. Don't hold your breath! To get the most benefit from your stretching hold each for a minimum of 30 seconds. You don't benefit much if your stretches are much less than this.

Different types of stretches

There are many, many different types of stretches, some of which are relevant to runners and some of which are not. Here we have included some of the most relevant with illustrations to show you how to perform them. They are not just for your legs but for all over your body. Flexibility in all of your core muscle groups is extremely important and will help your running performance.

Hamstrings (thigh – back)

Lie on your back and raise the knee of one leg. Hold the leg with two hands – one above and one below the knee joint. Pull the leg into the chest and slowly straighten the leg. Repeat with the other leg.

Figure 5.1 Hamstring stretch

Quadriceps (thigh – front)

Stand on one leg with the other leg pulled up to your behind, holding the front of the raised foot. Make sure that there is a slight bend in the leg on which you are standing. Keep your knees together and maintain an upright posture. Repeat with the other leg.

Figure 5.2 Quadriceps stretch

Calf (lower leg – back)

Lean into a wall and take the weight off one leg. Keep the other leg straight and lean into the stretch. Repeat with the other leg.

Figure 5.3 Calf stretch

Glutes (buttocks)

Lie on your back on the floor, bend your knees and place one ankle across the opposite thigh. Hold the other leg behind your thigh and pull into your body. Repeat with the other leg.

Figure 5.4 Glutes stretch

Hip flexors (pelvis – front)

Kneel on the floor with a cushion under the knees. Hold one foot and pull up towards the buttock while pushing your hips forwards and upwards. Repeat with the other leg.

Figure 5.5 Hip flexor stretch

Adductors (inside top of legs)

Sit with your back firmly against a wall and with your backside right up against the wall. Put the soles of your feet together. Slowly press down on the knees until you can feel the stretch, while keeping an upright posture at all times.

Figure 5.6 Adductor stretch

Back

Kneel on the floor and drop your chin to your chest. Push forward from your shoulders and arch your back.

Figure 5.7 Back stretch

Chest

Sit on the floor and stretch your arms out behind your back. Bend forward slowly with your head up. Push your chest forward further to get the most from the stretch.

Figure 5.8 Chest stretch

Shoulder

Put one arm out straight in front of you and bring it back across the chest and other shoulder. Holding with the other hand, gently pull it back further to maximize the stretch. Repeat with the other shoulder.

Figure 5.9 Shoulder stretch

The importance of entering events

Running on your own or with a couple of others during training is totally different from running with thousands of others on race day. That might sound blindingly obvious but many, many runners do nothing about it and turn up on race day and are promptly overwhelmed by the whole experience. Although nothing quite replicates the atmosphere of a major city-centre marathon you can go someway to preparing for it.

The really big marathons, like London, act as the centrepiece for running events all over their respective countries. Every year 10 km and half marathons are positioned in the national race calendar to take advantage of the thousands of runners training for the big one. It is vital that you take advantage of these events and get used to the experience of a big crowd. Although on a much smaller scale, you can get used to the pre-race tension, the preparation, the buzz of the start area, running with thousands of others and the excitement of the finish.

Nothing will prepare you for the feeling when you arrive at the start area of a major marathon. However, some big warm-up events can help prevent you being overcome by the first hour at a major, so get some practise under your belt!

Training with others

Running a marathon involves a huge amount of training and for many runners it is a very lonely experience. As with most things, there are of course two ways of looking at it.

For many runners it is a chance to spend some quality time on their own. With such busy work schedules it can be difficult to get time to yourself, but running gives you this. Work, personal issues, whatever it is, running gives you time to think things through and by the end of a run you can often have sorted out problems that you otherwise might not have had time to deal with.

Some runners, however, just do not want to run on their own and always seek the company of others. Running with others does seem to make the time go more quickly, which is why so many prefer this to solo running! It can also act as a motivator. Arranging to meet someone else for a run can often be the difference between going and not going. It's easy to think to yourself that you won't go today you'll leave it until tomorrow, but when you are going to meet someone else it is much harder to put it off. Running with others can also improve your performance, although it can of course work the other way as well. Ideally you should run with someone who is a little bit faster than you – not much – and then you will lift your performance. If, on the other hand, you run with someone slower than you then your development could be hindered as you will find yourself constantly holding yourself back.

Ideally you should combine solo runs with running with others. It is good to run on your own and have quality time to think and to develop your own pace, but it is also good to be able to chat to others in a more social context. Running doesn't need to be a lonely sport – but it does give you choice, unlike many pastimes. You can do whatever suits you.

Joining a running club

The same principles apply to joining a running club. If you prefer running on your own then a running club may not be your best option. However, even if you are a solo runner a running club can offer coaching facilities and access to experienced runners who could really help your running performance. They are also great places to meet other like-minded people, which may help your social life. Club nights and club trips to events are an important part of many runners' social calendar.

It is important if you do decide to join a running club to be committed to it. You will need to get involved and not simply buy a running vest and turn up to events. One of the financial benefits of belonging to a club is a reduction in the cost of entering events and many runners use membership for this purpose. If you get involved in the club you will get much more out of it.

Keeping a log

During your training for your first marathon you will run hundreds of miles. Keeping a record of these miles can be a great motivator in many ways, not least to chart your progress over the weeks and months.

There are many different types of logs available: some are specially designed computer programmes that allow you to record miles, time, weather conditions and with space to add comments; others are simply paper-based manual logs. With the growth of websites the weblog or 'blog' – a new concept – has become the preferred way forward for thousands of runners.

Blogs are interactive and allow others to make comments, which act as real encouragement when times get tough. Your blog is your own web page and you control exactly what is posted. They can vary, but generally speaking if you don't want to accept comments from others then you don't have to. Each day, week or month, depending on how often you want to post, you record your running training. You write as you feel, outlining how your training is progressing, including exactly what you want. The levels of feedback from others will very much depend on your style and how much you input into other people's blogs. Before long you could find yourself in a real community and that could play a major role in your motivation as the days pass.

There are hundreds of blogs on the realbuzz.com website and it is well worth a look here to see how others update the community on their training.

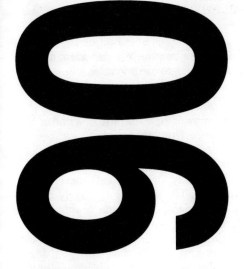

06

your marathon training plan

In this chapter you will learn:
- the importance of running at different speeds
- the importance of starting slowly
- the importance of the long run
- the importance of regular rest.

Tip at the top

The training plan is a guide to your training. You can adapt it to suit your circumstances, but stick to the principles.

It is a very bad idea to train for your first marathon without a training plan. You need guidance from those who have been through it before and who are qualified to make the whole experience a more pleasant one. Training plans are broken down into weeks and for each day of the week there is a recommended amount of training. There will be relatively little at the start, and then as the weeks pass, the amount of time that you spend on your feet increases. Each week the long run also increases, although as with all aspects of the plan, there will be periods of consolidation. There will also be days allocated for rest and it is as important that you stick to these as it is to follow the running days closely.

The plan is a guide and you should not be too concerned if you do not follow it to the letter. It is the principles that you must follow, i.e. slow progression, with regular long runs and rest days.

Below is a beginner's training plan from realbuzz.com that has been successfully followed by thousands of runners. It is aimed at runners who are looking to get round in four and a half to five and a half hours. It assumes that you are able to run for 15 minutes. If you are not able to do 15 minutes there is a six-week preparation guide that you should complete before starting the main marathon training programme. With that included this is a 30-week schedule.

Training pace guide

Use the following guide to understand the training listed within the plan.

Type of training run	Intensity index 1 = very easy 10 = very hard	Description
Super slow	2	Very, very, slow!
Easy jog	3	Easy, relaxed pace
Jog	4	Slighty faster but still easy
Comfortable	5	Faster than a jog but still comfortable
Steady	6	Even paced but you can start to feel it's getting harder
Brisk	7	Not a sprint but challenging!

Six-week preparation plan

Week 1

Day	Training	Notes
Mon	superslow 3 mins	Walk parts if you don't feel you can run all of it.
Tues	rest	
Wed	superslow 3 mins	Walk parts if you don't feel you can run all of it.
Thur	rest	
Fri	easy 4 mins	Walk parts if you don't feel you can run all of it.
Sat	rest	
Sun	rest	Walk parts if you don't feel you can run all of it.

Week 2

Day	Training	Notes
Mon	easy 5 mins	Walk parts if you don't feel you can run all of it.
Tues	rest	
Wed	easy 6 mins	Walk parts if you don't feel you can run all of it.
Thur	rest	
Fri	easy 6 mins	Walk parts if you don't feel you can run all of it.
Sat	rest	
Sun	rest	Walk parts if you don't feel you can run all of it.

Week 3

Day	Training	Notes
Mon	easy 7 mins	Try and keep walking to a minimum.
Tues	rest	
Wed	easy 8 mins	Try and keep walking to a minimum.
Thur	rest	
Fri	easy 8 mins	Try and keep walking to a minimum.
Sat	rest	
Sun	rest	Try and keep walking to a minimum.

Week 4

Day	Training	Notes
Mon	7 mins jog	Remember to breathe nice and deeply and stay relaxed.
Tues	rest	
Wed	8 mins jog	
Thur	rest	
Fri	8 mins jog	
Sat	rest	
Sun	9 mins jog	

Week 5

Day	Training	Notes
Mon	comfortable 7 mins	Remember to breathe nice and deeply and stay relaxed.
Tues	rest	
Wed	8 mins jog	
Thur	rest	
Fri	comfortable 8 mins	
Sat	rest	
Sun	rest	

Week 6

Day	Training	Notes
Mon	10 mins jog	Remember to breathe nice and deeply and stay relaxed.
Tues	rest	
Wed	11 mins jog	
Thur	rest	
Fri	11 mins jog	
Sat	rest	
Sun	12 mins jog	

Main marathon plan

Week 1

Day	Training	Notes
Mon	15 mins easy	Take walking break if needed.
Tues	rest	
Wed	15 mins easy	Take walking break if needed.
Thur	rest	
Fri	15–20 mins easy	Take walking break if needed.
Sat	rest	
Sun	20 mins easy	Take walking break if needed.

Week 2

Day	Training	Notes
Mon	rest	
Tues	15 mins easy	
Wed	rest	
Thur	20 mins easy	
Fri	rest	
Sat	rest	
Sun	25 mins easy	Take walking break if needed.

Week 3

Day	Training	Notes
Mon	rest	
Tues	25 mins easy	
Wed	rest	
Thur	30 mins easy	
Fri	rest	
Sat	rest	
Sun	35 mins easy	Try and run non-stop if you can.

Week 4

Day	Training	Notes
Mon	10–15 mins very easy	
Tues	25 mins steady	
Wed	rest	
Thur	25 mins steady	
Fri	rest	
Sat	rest	
Sun	35 mins easy	Repeat of last Sunday but try and improve the distance covered.

Week 5

Day	Training	Notes
Mon	10–15 mins very easy	
Tues	rest	
Wed	25–30 mins steady	
Thur	rest	
Fri	25 mins easy	
Sat	rest	
Sun	40 mins jog/walk	Try and run as much as you can but walk if needed.

Week 6

Day	Training	Notes
Mon	20 mins recovery easy jog	
Tues	25 mins steady	
Wed	rest	
Thur	35 mins steady	
Fri	rest	
Sat	rest	
Sun	40 mins jog	Try and run without stopping.

Week 7

Day	Training	Notes
Mon	20 mins recovery easy jog	
Tues	25 mins steady	
Wed	rest	
Thur	35–40 mins steady	
Fri	rest	
Sat	10 mins very easy jog	
Sun	50 mins slow	Walk occasionally if needed.

Week 8

Your first event – 10 km.

Day	Training	Notes
Mon	rest	
Tues	25–30 mins steady	
Wed	rest	
Thur	25–30 mins steady	
Fri	rest	
Sat	10 mins very easy jog	
Sun	10 km road race	Do not go off too quickly, and enjoy it!

Week 9

Day	Training	Notes
Mon	15 mins jog	
Tues	40 mins steady	
Wed	rest	
Thur	35–40 mins	
Fri	rest	
Sat	15 mins very easy jog	
Sun	60–75 mins very easy	Walk occasionally if needed.

Week 10

Day	Training	Notes
Mon	rest	
Tues	40 mins steady	
Wed	rest	
Thur	50 mins comfortable	
Fri	rest	
Sat	15 mins very easy jog	
Sun	75 mins comfortable	Walk occasionally if needed but less than last week.

Week 11

Day	Training	Notes
Mon	20 mins easy recovery	
Tues	40 mins steady	
Wed	rest	
Thur	50 mins easy	
Fri	rest	
Sat	rest	
Sun	80–90 mins	Take regular walking breaks.

Week 12

Day	Training	Notes
Mon	20 mins easy recovery	
Tues	40 mins steady	
Wed	rest	
Thur	rest	
Fri	40 mins brisk pace	
Sat	rest	
Sun	90–100 mins	Take regular walking breaks. Start taking water with you.

Week 13

Day	Training	Notes
Mon	rest	
Tues	50 mins steady	
Wed	rest	
Thur	40 mins steady	
Fri	20 mins steady	
Sat	rest	
Sun	100–110 mins easy	Try and walk less on this run.

Week 14

Day	Training	Notes
Mon	rest	
Tues	20 mins steady	
Wed	65 mins easy	
Thur	rest	
Fri	40 mins easy	
Sat	rest	
Sun	120 mins very easy	Very slow and with water.

Week 15

Your second event – half marathon.

Day	Training	Notes
Mon	rest	
Tues	30–35 mins steady	
Wed	30 mins steady	
Thur	rest	
Fri	rest	
Sat	10 mins jog	Just to loosen up.
Sun	half marathon	This is a training run, not a race!

Week 16

Day	Training	Notes
Mon	10–20 mins recovery	
Tues	rest	
Wed	30 mins steady	
Thur	60 mins brisk	
Fri	rest	
Sat	30 mins jog	
Sun	120 mins comfortable	

Week 17

Day	Training	Notes
Mon	30 mins easy	
Tues	rest	
Wed	60 mins brisk	Try and improve on the distance covered last Wed.
Thur	rest	
Fri	40 mins steady	
Sat	rest	
Sun	130–140 mins very easy	Take it very slowly.

Week 18

Day	Training	Notes
Mon	rest	
Tues	40 mins steady	
Wed	rest	
Thur	75 mins comfortable pace	
Fri	20 mins jog	
Sat	rest	
Sun	140–150 mins very easy	Take it very slowly.

Week 19

Day	Training	Notes
Mon	10–20 mins recovery jog	
Tues	40 mins steady	
Wed	rest	
Thur	75 mins comfortable pace	
Fri	rest	
Sat	30 mins easy pace	
Sun	150–160 mins comfortable	Don't start too quickly.

Week 20

Day	Training	Notes
Mon	30 mins easy pace	
Tues	rest	
Wed	50 mins fast	
Thur	rest	
Fri	50 mins easy	
Sat	rest	
Sun	180 mins slow	Don't start too quickly.

Week 21

PEAK WEEK!

Day	Training	Notes
Mon	20 mins jog recovery	
Tues	40 mins brisk	
Wed	rest	
Thur	60 mins steady	
Fri	rest	
Sat	rest	
Sun	200 mins slow	Your last long run.

Week 22

Taper time.

Day	Training	Notes
Mon	20 mins slow jog or rest	
Tues	30 mins brisk	
Wed	rest	
Thur	50 mins steady	
Fri	rest	
Sat	rest	
Sun	120 mins steady	

Week 23

Taper time.

Day	Training	Notes
Mon	20 mins easy	
Tues	rest	
Wed	40 mins easy	
Thur	rest	
Fri	rest	
Sat	10 mins jog	
Sun	70 mins in race kit and shoes	

Week 24

RACE WEEK!

Day	Training	Notes
Mon	30 mins jog	
Tues	rest	
Wed	20 mins jog	
Thur	rest	
Fri	rest	
Sat	10 mins very, very easy jog	
Sun	race day	

07

the importance of the gym

In this chapter you will learn:
- how to cross train
- about winter alternatives
- about gyms that have their own running clubs.

Tip at the top

Don't be scared about heading to the gym. Most people are at the same level and are focussed on their goals. Don't worry about what others are thinking.

If the words 'the gym' fill you with dread, they shouldn't. If you're a member of a gym already then you're a long way down the marathon training road already.

Using a gym is an important part of a marathon plan for a number of reasons. If you are uncomfortable at the thought of heading to a gym then you shouldn't be. They are probably not what you think, so put your misconceptions behind you and make what will prove to be a vital step on the marathon road. Gyms are generally not full of body builders, and if your nearest one is then it's not the place for you. You need a gym with a range of fitness equipment, including plenty of treadmills, rowing machines, bikes, steppers and a selection of fixed weights machines. What you don't want is a huge area devoted to free weights dominated by huge steroid-driven monsters attempting to out perform their neighbour. If that's what your local gym has then find something else. There aren't many around like that anyway these days as the market has changed and it has changed to the market that you are in – the general fitness market, which includes runners.

Most gyms are frequented not by body builders, but by normal, everyday people, the majority of whom are trying to lose weight, often joining in the New Year to shed unwanted winter pounds accumulated in the dark months when exercise can prove difficult. Gyms are full of average people all working individually but ultimately collectively for a common purpose. Many have more specialist targets and many seem to have no targets at all, preferring to chat rather than work. The atmosphere can prove intimidating for the first few days but after a while you will soon settle in and it will seem much more of a natural place to spend time. You must, however, give it time.

Allow yourself time to settle in and feel comfortable, but even more importantly you must allow time for the benefits to take effect. Many people join a gym and expect miracles within a couple of weeks. When these miracles don't materialize – and they won't – the temptation is to quit. What most people don't realize is that changes are taking place to your body, often under layers of fat which will eventually be lost. It is then that the results of all the hard work become visible. For many people that stage never becomes reality, primarily because of their impatience. If you join a gym for cross training, muscle endurance, general weight loss or to use the treadmill, give it time and you will eventually see the benefits.

If you are concerned about the cost of going to the gym, don't be. You don't necessarily need to join a gym, you can often 'pay as you go' at many of them, particularly those operated by local authorities. If you do decide to join don't assume that they are prohibitively expensive. It is a highly competitive market these days and there are always deals to be had. If you can go at lunchtime you will often get 'off-peak' memberships, which can be excellent value if you are prepared to stay away from busy periods like early evenings. Privately operated gyms are also a good option, with good deals and excellent service often the norm. Don't always go with the advertised price. If you don't ask for a better deal then you won't get one.

Why should a runner, and especially one training for a marathon, need to go to the gym? There are plenty of reasons, some obvious, some not so obvious.

Essential for cross training

As we discussed in the chapter on training, cross training is an essential part of the modern marathon runner's programme. Frowned upon by the traditionalist, cross training is widely accepted as vital in the development of the new type of runner; the runner who needs to introduce fitness back into their lifestyle.

Cross training can be done outside the gym, as most people have access to a bike, a piece of fitness equipment at home or live fairly near a pool, but it is a lot easier if you can get to a gym. Decent gyms will have a range of equipment in an atmosphere that is designed to make cross training easier and more enjoyable than being at home or out on a bike in the middle of winter in the dark. Importantly, cross training works far more effectively if you move quickly from one piece of equipment to another, so maintaining your heart rate at the correct level. This is far easier to do at a gym than at home and it is the right environment for it. Keeping your heart rate at the optimum level builds endurance and burns fat, but only if it is kept in the right zone for the right amount of time. With equipment in close proximity this can be achieved in the gym and you reach your goals. Gyms are designed with your goals as their core focus and this is one reason why you will see all the cardiovascular (CV) gear so close together.

Not only is the gym the perfect place for the CV component of your training but it is also the right place for the muscle endurance element of it. Muscular endurance, which builds stamina in your muscles, is the type of muscle work that runners need, whereas muscle strength work just builds bulk, which you don't need. Adding this training into your programme will give you a more balanced approach to running and will ensure that your body gets more tone and less of the 'classic runner' physique. This type of muscle workout is difficult at home, unless you invest in a range of equipment, but easy in a gym as it will have already invested in the right gear for you. Hamstring curls, among other types of exercise, which may seem a bit alien to you now, will become second nature if you join a gym. You will give yourself stamina in your muscles which will make your running easier and, importantly, will help with injury prevention, which is of great importance.

Your home is many things but in most cases it is not a fitness centre. It is far better to pack a bag and head to the gym for a decent all-round workout than to try to replicate one in front of the TV. There is nothing wrong with having fitness equipment at home in case you can't get to the gym, but don't rely on using it very often. How many people hang their clothes on their static bike in the bedroom, rather than using it for the purpose that it was originally intended, or keep falling over the set of dumbbells that never get used!

A cold-weather alternative

Running in cold weather is not easy however motivated you are and it is made even more difficult when you have to do it in the dark! Worse still are icy and snowy conditions when you shouldn't run at all because it is too dangerous and could cause you serious injury. On days when it's not wise to venture out or you just don't feel like braving the elements there is an alternative.

Instead of putting on three layers of clothes and getting chilled to the core why not head to the gym instead and take advantage of some treadmill training. The usual complaint about treadmills is that they are boring, but give them a chance and you'll soon find out that they have a host of benefits.

The first is that they allow you to stick to your training plan however bad conditions are outside. There is absolutely no excuse to stop when you have access to a treadmill. Whatever your plan requires you can do it if you head to the gym. You will be able to run in shorts and a t-shirt or running vest and enjoy the conditions rather than battle against the elements. While running in tough conditions can be very rewarding at times, it can be soul destroying to have to do it day after day. The gym gives you a very viable alternative.

The second benefit is that it can help to prevent injuries. Hitting the roads relentlessly can potentially cause damage to knees, hips, shins and many other parts of your body, but using the treadmill regularly can help to minimize this impact. Not all runners get injuries, but many do succumb to niggles at some stage. The treadmill, unlike the road, has significant shock absorption benefits and can noticeably reduce the impact on your joints. However, you should not have an exclusively treadmill-based programme as your body will not be suitably adapted for running on the road.

In an ideal world you should combine the road with the treadmill, even when conditions outside are suitable for running. This will go a long way to helping avoid annoying injuries that can cost you time during your training.

A third benefit of treadmill training is the availability of monitoring information. You may not be concerned about speed in the early days – and you shouldn't be – but it is always helpful to know at what pace you are running so you can benchmark your progress over time. It's not something that you should be overly concerned about it in the early stages, but it will become a real motivator as time passes. Without even trying you will gradually get faster without realizing it. Running on the road can make monitoring more difficult unless you have the most expensive speed and distance monitor, but with a treadmill read-out right in front of you, information is always at your fingertips. Furthermore, you can increase or decrease your pace immediately and know exactly how far you will run as a result. Each week you can aim to slightly increase your pace, safe in the knowledge that this will be building your stamina.

To some treadmills are boring, but to others they can make all the difference to their marathon training programme.

Running clubs

We've had a good look at running clubs in the training chapter, but it is worth pointing out that many gyms have running clubs for members and they can quite often be ideal for runners, especially beginners, embarking on a marathon training programme. There are pros and cons, of course with these clubs, but generally they are worth getting involved with. At least you know it's one or two less runs a week that you need to worry about – someone else is doing the thinking!

In the early stages of your training make sure that you are not out of your depth. Sometimes the clubs have a fixed five- or six-mile course each week and run at a certain pace, which may be a bit more than you are up to at that time. You will get there but make sure you are ready. Also check if they do reps and interval work along the way (these are covered in the training chapter). If they do and you're not ready for that, don't worry – you don't need to join in. Remember that these groups aren't always operated by gym instructors with any real running coaching experience so don't necessarily expect tuition, just a supervised run. You may get lucky and find someone with some real running pedigree, but don't assume that you will.

An ideal social environment

Another benefit of running clubs within the gym and the gym environment itself is the social element. Running a marathon is a lonely occupation and it is good to have others around you doing the same. Chat when you're out running together about the challenges that you're facing and you may find it all becomes a bit easier when you can help each other through it.

It is quite common to meet potential training partners at the gym, which can make all the difference to your marathon preparation. Some runners prefer to hit the streets on their own and others prefer to meet the challenge with the support of a partner. If you fit into the latter category then you may well strike lucky at the gym.

Even if you don't spend much time chatting in the gym, it's good to feel part of a busy gym environment. You may keep yourself to yourself but it's quietly reassuring to know that you are training alongside many others who are doing the same thing.

Whatever your preference you will often find the company of others, whether you are communicating or not, can make your marathon training seem a lot easier.

If you haven't really bought into the gym idea up to this point then be prepared to have another look, but with a really open mind. If you have tried it in the past and have had a bad experience, don't worry, it is probably a one-off and if you try somewhere else you may well find that your views change considerably. If you can't find an alternative then give your original choice another go and think of the positives discussed above. If you've never been to the gym then you ought to give it a go as soon as you can. It could give your marathon training the edge that it needs, especially if you have winter training to contend with!

08

eating and drinking

In this chapter you will learn:
- about the food groups that are vital to your running
- how to fuel your race training
- what to eat and drink on race day.

Tip at the top

Make sure you have a healthy, balanced diet and drink plenty of water. Eat little and often and don't eat junk, even though you may crave it!

Many things will change in your life during your marathon training, among them your nutritional requirements. You will develop eating and drinking habits that you will laugh about when it's all over, including a dependence on pasta of near addict proportions!

The more you train, the more fuel your body demands and generally speaking this comes from carbohydrates, fat and protein. As you progress over the months from complete beginner to regular runner so your energy needs increase. For every mile that you run you will burn around 100 calories, so clearly changes to eating patterns may be required. Your craving for carbohydrates will hit peak levels, especially as you near your long run around three weeks before marathon day. However, it is not all about carbohydrates and you must ensure that you eat a healthy, balanced diet throughout your running career.

Different foods contain different amounts of carbohydrate, fat and protein and each is broken down by the body to provide a different level of energy per gram of food. This is measured in kilocalories and surprisingly it is fats that release far more energy than carbohydrates – 9 kilocalories per gram compared with 3.75! Proteins release 4 kilocalories per gram. Unfortunately this doesn't mean that fats are the best energy fuel – they aren't. Glucose, which is stored in the body as glycogen, is the best option and this is created when carbohydrates are broken down. In the ideal world your glycogen stores would be limitless but unfortunately this is not the case, hence the need to eat the right foods to ensure that these stores are replenished regularly.

The amount of fluids that you consume will also hit new highs during your training, so it is important that you develop a strategy to deal with these new requirements.

During training

Food groups

Talk to any runner about nutrition and chances are the conversation will turn to carbohydrates very quickly. This is understandable given all the hype about this particular food group, but it is important to realize that nutrition during your training is not all about how much pasta you can eat!

Marathon training is aerobic exercise, which means that your body will use carbohydrates, proteins and fats, but it is the carbohydrates that progressively will be used more. There are a number of factors that dictate the relative amounts that are used, including your fitness levels, the intensity of the exercise and the length of the session. In the early days you will burn a higher percentage of fat because your fitness level will be lower, your sessions will be short and they will not be too intense. As your training increases, so the proportion of fat against glucose changes significantly and this is why you must adjust your diet as your training programme changes. The good news is that the more you train and the higher the intensity the more calories you burn! Without regular consumption of carbohydrates you will not be able to train effectively, as you will feel constantly tired and devoid of energy. Eat complex carbohydrates and you will feel much stronger.

Complex carbohydrates are the key to generating energy as they release the fuel you need very slowly into your body. This more sustainable energy is the complete opposite of the type generated by biscuits, chocolate and the like, which although you might prefer the taste, aren't good for you in the long term. They are notoriously high in calories and may contribute to some beginners actually putting on weight rather than losing it. You will feel more hungry than normal when you train regularly and you should satisfy this hunger with complex carbohydrates such as bread, pasta, potatoes and rice. As with all things, however, eat them in moderation. Running is not an excuse to eat as much as possible!

Just after you return from a run it is important to refuel as quickly as possible, so stock up at home with plenty of glucose drinks. For a few minutes after training your muscles will crave carbohydrates and you will also need to ensure you have the right levels of fluids. By taking on board one of these drinks you will satisfy both requirements.

Don't, however, become obsessed with carbohydrates to the detriment of other food groups. It is important to ensure that you have balanced meals with plenty of protein and unsaturated fats. It's not just those trying to build muscle who need proteins, it is also runners. Muscles are damaged during training and it is proteins that help repair them. Aim to eat between one and two grams of protein per day per kilogram of bodyweight. Fats have a very bad reputation, some of which is deserved and some of which is most definitely not. There are good fats (unsaturated fats) and bad fats (saturated fats), with the latter generally coming from animals, for example diary products. As well as being an energy source, good fats can have a number of health benefits, so ignore them at your peril. The good fats include olive oil, which you can easily incorporate into your diet in a variety of innovative ways. While unsaturated fats have health benefits, saturated fats can cause major problems, including heart disease. Stroke and angina are linked to the clogging of artery walls from excessive levels of cholesterol. So how much fat should you consume? Balance is always the key but look to focus on the unsaturated fats, which are predominantly from plants. Government recommendations for saturated fats – the bad ones – are that they should make up no more than 10 per cent of your total energy intake, which works out at 28 g a day for men and 22 g for women. Your total fat intake should be no more than 35 per cent of your total energy intake daily – 70 g for a woman and 100 g for men.

Before your run

Before you start your run you must make sure that you have eaten enough to give you the required energy levels. This is a particular issue with the long run which is the key component of your marathon training. Many runners do their long run at the weekend and often fairly early in the morning to get the most from their day, so in many cases the most important meal of the day – breakfast – is missed. To tackle a long run with no food in the tank is a big mistake and it will often result in a poor run. You must fuel accordingly. The same applies to evening runs. If you've missed lunch don't consider going for a run after work until you have had something to eat. It need not be a big meal, just a snack, but you must eat something that is going to give you the required energy. On the flip side, do not eat too close to your run. If you are waiting until after your main meal before running then you will need to leave at least two to two and a half hours before you run. There is nothing worse for your running than heading out on a full stomach. You will feel sluggish and you will not enjoy your run.

During your run

As your runs get longer so you will find it important to take some food or drink with you. The options are now extremely varied with one of the best being energy gels or bars. On a long run you will burn a large number of calories and deplete your energy stores, which as a result will need constant replenishment. Gels or bars are a quick way of absorbing complex carbohydrate and as a result give you increased energy levels. Energy drinks that are full of glucose have the same effect. Gels have a thick syrupy consistency and need in most cases to be taken with water. They come in small sachets and should be taken in small amounts at a time. The best approach is to rip off the top take a sip and then take some water. Do not take it all down in one go and always take water unless the manufacturer has advised that this is not needed. Taking gels too quickly can cause sickness so be cautious, especially in the early days of using them. There are a large number on the market and it is worth experimenting until you find one that you really get on with. Once you find that one then stick with it.

During the course of a marathon you will need around four of these, so adjust downwards to suit your long runs. You can buy belts that are especially designed to carry gels and in many cases water bottles as well. Also available are small flasks which can hold around four of the gels. These products can be quite messy and sticky, but with a flask that issue is significantly reduced. Energy bars are another option and are preferred by many runners, principally because of the taste. They are, however, a little more cumbersome to carry and you will generally need a few more to replicate the effect of the gels, which are a much more concentrated shot of carbohydrate.

These products are an important supplement to your diet but it is important that you do not become reliant on them. They are perfect for training runs but do not regard them as a substitute for a healthy diet. There will be many occasions when you will feel tired, and when this happens you must eat properly and do not reach for an energy gel to give you a lift. Take fruit with you to work, rather than these synthetic products. If you eat well and make sure you have a balanced diet, containing the correct proportions of carbohydrates, fat and protein you have no need for supplements. If you have a current requirement for them such as the use of iron supplements by some vegetarians then carry on, but don't head to the chemist and stock up on vitamins and minerals because you think your body will need them. Eat well and your body will have everything it needs from your food.

Food will become something of an obsession as your training progresses and you will feel like eating pretty much all of the time. This is okay as long as you don't eat too much at a time. 'Grazing' is a very important part of marathon training. Small, regular meals are the best way to eat and by taking breakfast cereal, fruit or nuts with you to work you will find hunger is kept at bay and the weight will stay off. Eat too much at a time, the weight will go on and you will feel sluggish. Eat little and often.

Drinking

Your drinking habits will alter dramatically over time and is important that you adapt accordingly. During your normal working life you should be drinking around 1.5 litres of water a day, but as your training progress you will need to increase this to around two to two and a half litres depending on the run that you have planned for that day. Make sure that you have access to good clean water and always have some on hand in your workplace, in the house or in the car. Make sure that you always drink well after a run and as the length of the run increases you should start to take some with you. Don't start taking water with you too soon however. All too often a beginner's running style will be damaged by carrying heavy water bottles far too early in their careers. You do not need to take water on runs of less than an hour, particularly in the middle of winter. Hydrate well during the day and you will be fine to run for at least an hour and in most cases a lot longer. Taking water on long runs can be difficult but there are ways of doing it. Go out in the car first and place some at strategic locations or have someone meet you on the way if you can. If all else fails then buy one of the many nutrition belts available and take it with you. Avoid carrying a bottle in your hands if you possibly can.

Monitoring

As the weeks of your training pass you will develop an eating and drinking pattern that suits your metabolism and your running. There is no particular right and wrong way to the perfect nutrition programme for your body, just a set of guidelines that will help you find it. Follow these and you will find the fuel to drive you through the many, many training runs that prepare you for the big day.

You must always carefully monitor your weight and ensure that your calorie intake near enough matches your calorie expenditure. If you don't then one of two things can happen. First, if you take in more than you expend you will gain weight and, second, if you expend more than you take in then weight loss will occur. While most of us want this to happen you do not want it to go too far. Don't become obsessed with losing weight, especially too quickly. This will be bad for your health and can cause long-term problems. Your weight loss should be long term and sustainable. If you feel it is getting out of control then have a chat to a nutritionist and get a professional opinion on the situation.

Race week

Race week is the most unusual of your whole training programme. You will run very little and eat a lot. But how much should you eat?

Most beginners will have heard of the term 'carbo-loading', but what is it all about and how much should you load? It is literally filling up with fuel, which is then stored ready for use on race day. Because only a certain amount can be stored by the body, there is only a certain amount that you should eat. Go above this figure and you have no real benefit on the day.

In the first half of race week eat normally and make sure that you are still drinking around two litres of water a day. When you get to the last three days before the event you should start to be a bit more scientific about your carbohydrate consumption. The amount that you consume is measured according to your weight in kilograms, so before you do anything make sure that you know what that is in race week. Once you have that you should multiply that figure by the amount of carbohydrate that you require per kilogramme, which for a marathon is eight to ten grams a day. If for example you weigh 11 to 12 stones this is 64 to 70 kg and if you multiple that by eight to ten grams of carbohydrates a day then you will need 560 to 700 g a day.

To give you an idea of how to eat that much carbohydrate, a medium bread slice is 15 g, a banana 20 g and a large jacket potato up to 100 g. That is a lot of food and of course you must spread it out over the course of the day, 'grazing' as much as possible. It is likely that you will feel pretty bloated and not especially comfortable, but it won't be for long and it will all be worth it on race day, especially in the last ten or so miles.

Although the focus should be on carbohydrates, make sure that you do also eat some proteins and unsaturated fats during race week.

The race

Many, many runners' first experience of the marathon distance is ruined because, after all the months of planning, it goes horribly wrong on race day. Often race day goes wrong because of a mistake with the approach to nutrition.

It is vital that you eat breakfast, are well hydrated before and during the race and do not take too many energy drinks or gels on the way round. Get those three elements right and the day should go well. Get them wrong and chances are that it won't.

It is very likely that you will have an early start on race day. Some events require you to be at the start two or three hours beforehand, although an hour and a half is more than sufficient for the Flora London Marathon where you can make your own way to the start. For this event you should be there for around 8.30 a.m. which for most people means a six to six thirty wake-up call. If you eat nothing between then and race finish which will be 1 p.m. onwards and you will have problems. Your body simply will not have enough fuel and you will probably hit the dreaded 'wall' when your glycogen stores are totally depleted. You must make sure you eat something, but not too much or else you will have a whole new set of other problems. The perfect breakfast is tea or coffee, dry toast and a banana, but only if you are used to all of these elements. Just as you should try nothing new in race week, so you should definitely try nothing new on race day. If you always have a particular muesli bar before a long run then stick with it. Don't try a different brand, go with what you know. Make sure that you drink water in the lead-up to the start, but not too much. Around a litre in the two or three hours beforehand is enough. You do not want to spend too long in the toilet queues. The same goes for eating too much at breakfast. If you go for a full cooked option you could have trouble just before the start. Remember, if you eat large quantities of food in the build-up it may well want to come out beforehand or even worse, during the race!

Take some food with you to the start if you think you'll need it, like bananas or bagels, and do not assume you will be able to buy them onsite. You might be able to but leave nothing to chance. This also applies to water. Whatever you think you need, make sure that you take it with you.

Make sure that you know exactly how often the water and energy products are available along the route and if you think you need more make sure you have enough with you. If you are running one of the major marathons like London you will not need anything. These events have medical directors and they will ensure that your nutrition requirements are met around the course. In London there are water stations at every mile – from three miles onwards – and energy drink stations every five miles – from the five-mile mark onwards. Many weeks beforehand you should find out the particular brand of energy drink that your event is using on race day and train with it. They are all different and you must make sure that your body is used to the specific brand available at your race. Do not train with one and then use another on race day or you could face some significant stomach problems. If you have trained with a specific brand and you are happy with it then take some with you for race day. Do not switch at the last minute.

During the race you should take sips of water at every water station even if you do not feel like it. Don't drink too much, just a few sips and then discard the bottle carefully making sure you don't impede other runners in the process. If you become thirsty then you are dehydrated and it is difficult to recover from this problem during a marathon. Drink small quantities at every stop and you will not feel thirsty. The same goes for the energy drinks. Do not take on too much at any one time and make sure that you drink a small volume of water to dilute it. This will reduce the impact on the stomach. If you take an energy drink on board too quickly you could have unfortunate problems, which include digestion issues and vomiting. Take it slowly and with water. Just because you are given a certain volume, don't assume that you have to drink it all. Take small amounts and discard. The Flora London Marathon provides pouches of Lucozade energy drink which can be carried with you.

The benefit of this is that you can constantly sip from them and take the rest with you without spilling it everywhere.

Along the courses in big city-centre marathons, many of the watching crowd will offer you a wide range of food and drink. Treat this with a huge amount of caution. While it is unlikely you will have a problem you can never be sure, especially if the food is unwrapped or the drink unsealed. Products include boiled sweets, jelly babies, chocolate, bananas, oranges and much more. Think twice before taking anything – just in case. Only eat or drink anything that you can be sure of!

Post race

As soon as you get over the finish line you should think about nutrition. Although your emotions will be high you must not lose sight of your body's food and drink requirements, both in the moments immediately after the finish and in the few hours afterwards. Think about three key areas. First, you must rehydrate quickly. It is very likely that you will need to get fluid into your system as soon as you can and this is why most of the big marathons will provide water at the finish. Do not grab a bottle and drink it all straightaway, but instead start to sip it and carrying on sipping from it regularly for the next hour or so. Aim to drink about half a litre in the hour after you cross the finish line. This will give it time to be absorbed into your body.

Second, consume an energy drink. Again, most of the top events like London will have energy drinks available at the finish area to help you replenish your glycogen stores. Your glucose stores at this stage will be very low and you do need to get them back to reasonable levels quickly to help in the recovery process. In the minutes directly after the finish your body will be able to do this more effectively, but again sip the drink and do not take it down too quickly (if you do you may well bring it back up again). This will also help hydrate you and satisfy some of the hunger cravings that you may have. Avoid food straight after the finish and leave it at least an hour before tackling anything more than a sandwich. Also avoid alcohol for a few hours afterwards. It can have a much more immediate effect than normal and inhibit the rehydration process!

The third area that you need to consider in the hours after the race is the consumption of a balanced meal, which is rich in carbohydrates that can help restore your body to its pre-race levels. Although you may be too tired to even think about it you must aim to eat later that evening, but eat well. You may fancy some fast food, especially if you have resisted for many weeks while you have been training, but now is not the time. Eat well on race night and it will help you to recover.

Get your nutrition strategy right from the early days of your training to the hours after your big race and you are half way to a successful marathon debut!

09

the injury and illness curse

In this chapter you will learn:
- why you get injured
- about the different types of injury
- how to treat blisters.

Tip at the top

However difficult it is, you must never run while injured or when you are ill. Build in extra weeks on your training schedule just in case.

At some stage in your training it is very likely that you will be struck down by the dreaded injury and illness curse. Sometimes you can avoid it and sometimes you can't, but you can guarantee that it will be one of the most frustrating times of your running career. Most runners will pick up a minor injury as their body adjusts to the rigours of the new training regime, and with a bit of rest it will soon clear up, but occasionally you may fall victim to a more serious issue that could need lengthy treatment.

It is important that you always listen to your body and do not carry on regardless. Whatever your problem you have it for a reason and you need to deal with it. This may simply mean a couple of days' rest or a break because you have a cold, or a visit to a physiotherapist with a course of treatment. Rest is always the key and this is why training programmes are compiled in the way that they are. You must allow plenty of time to train for a marathon and build in some spare days or even weeks to allow for the days when you simply won't be able to run. Even if you are one of the lucky ones who is not afflicted by an injury or illness the rest will still do you good!

Why do injuries arise?

There are a number of reasons why you might pick up an injury during your marathon training, many of which you can do something about. These can be divided into your running training, your cross training and your shoes.

Running training

Your running training involves a number of different components each of which, if not carried out according to the plan, can play a role in the development of injuries. If you follow a training plan like the one in this book you will significantly reduce the chances of getting an injury from your running training because it has been written with injury prevention as a key priority. Many runners, especially beginners, do too much too soon and overload their body with exercise when it is not ready for it. Progression in your training is an absolute priority. You must allow your body to get used to the stresses that you are putting it under. This also applies to interval and speed work. It is easy to get carried away and up the pace by using sessions. If you are not ready for them, which many beginners aren't, or do them without supervision then there is a serious risk of injuries like stress fractures.

Always remember to take heed of the rest days in your plan. They are there for a reason. You must allow your body the chance to recover from the days that you do run. Even though you might not want to take a break you must. Think carefully about where you run and mix up your running surfaces. Too much road running and you may get the dreaded shin splints injury and too much running on uneven surfaces and you may damage muscles and tendons as they strive to keep you balanced. There is the also the problem of entering too many events. When you run in an event you will find that you run a lot faster than you do on a normal training run and if you do too many you will put too much pressure on your body. Often, inadequate rest leads to increased stress which results in injury. If you do get the event bug, try and manage it and make sure you take an extra day's rest after each race. Don't forget your warm up, cool down and stretching regime. The more flexible you are the less likely you are to pull a muscle.

Cross training

Your cross training regime can also lead to injuries. It is a great idea to cross train, in other words to use different types of exercise to improve your fitness, but you must be cautious. This is not such a problem with cardiovascular equipment like the stepper or rower, but you should seek assistance from a gym instructor before beginning a programme. Using the wrong technique on the rowing machine, for example, could cause you some serious problems. Most problems in the gym come from resistance training, where the wrong muscles are worked or certain muscles are worked too hard causing imbalances that lead to pulls.

Shoes

Your shoes can also be a cause of injuries. There are many different types of running shoes and you must make sure that you are properly fitted out at a specialist retailer before you start your training. If you wear a pair designed for someone with a particular running style that you don't have, you could develop a style that causes you problems. Also remember to change your shoes regularly. Depending on how you run you should expect a pair of shoes to last between 500 and 600 miles, and if you go well past that they will lose 'air' and consequently their ability to act as shock absorbers will be significantly diminished. Invest wisely in your shoes and you could well prevent a whole host of injuries.

Types of running injuries

There are two types of injuries of concern to runners.

The first type is a traumatic injury caused by a sudden incidence like falling over while running on the ice and breaking a leg, but thankfully these are usually quite rare. The second type, overuse injuries, are unfortunately not so rare. This sort of injury is caused by overloading tissue that has become damaged in some way. It is unlikely that you will notice the problem in the early days but over time the problem will get worse until it hurts too much to run on it.

There are two types of overuse injury: those that result from the way you are built and those that come about from external factors. The former can be your running style or your size, whereas the latter can include the injuries outlined above – not having enough rest, poor running shoes or running too much on the same surface.

Most injuries are a combination of these two types of overuse injury, and now that you know what they are you can do something to avoid them!

Coughs, colds, flu and other viruses

These can strike at any time, but do not be surprised if you are hit by a debilitating virus at some stage in your training. It is especially common in the depth of winter which, if you are training for London, could well be a crucial stage of your training schedule. If you are eating and drinking well and not overtraining this will help, but it is not unusual to fall victim to such an illness even if you doing everything you can to prevent it. If it strikes then you must stop running immediately and not restart until it is completely out of your system. If you start running again too quickly the problem will linger for much longer than it would have done if you had rested properly.

Viruses in particular can put real pressure on your heart and you must not run while you are ill. A head cold is a different issue, but even then you are well advised to stop running until it has cleared. If you are due to run an event and you are ill beforehand then you should not run. Race conditions will mean you are likely to run more quickly than normal which will put even more strain on your heart.

The more time you have given yourself to train the less important these enforced rest periods will have be. If you start your programme too late, a week or two illness break could seriously impact on your race day performance.

How to look after yourself

We've seen how you can become injured and the type of injuries that you can sustain, so how can you look after yourself to prevent these problems?

Invest in your kit

Worn shoes or the wrong shoes can cause injuries, so you need to spend time and money making sure that you get the right ones. Don't be tempted by cheap, bargain shoes – spend more on getting them right. You might only need to spend another £20 or so on the right shoes and this, over the life of the shoe, is a very small price to pay to help prevent injury. Don't listen to ill-advised high street sales staff in mass market sports shops who will often try and encourage you to buy the wrong shoes just to hit their sales quota; head to a specialist running shop and listen to what they tell you.

Heart-rate monitors are another important part of your kit and one that can most definitely help with injury prevention. Buy one and get to know it intimately. It will help you train in the right training zone, which means you are not running too hard.

This is especially important in the early days when it is easy to go off too quickly, and also as you gain in confidence and try too much speed work. Take note of the monitor and do not push yourself. Set the alarm so it sounds if you go outside the upper limit of your zone.

Eat and drink well

To maintain overall wellbeing throughout your training it is vital that you eat and drink well. You must stay hydrated and you must eat balanced meals, full of carbohydrates, protein and unsaturated fats. As you spend more time training so you must increase the amount of carbohydrate that you consume on a pro rata basis. There is more on this in Chapter 08. Without the right balance of food and drink you will become increasingly run down, your resistance to infection will increase and you could become ill.

Make sure that you stretch

In the training chapter you will find a programme of stretching exercises. Learn them and make sure that after every run, you spend at least 10 to 15 minutes stretching using the correct technique. This will improve your flexibility significantly and help prevent damage to your muscles, which if serious could put your running training on hold for many weeks. Tears to hamstrings, quadriceps and calf muscles are a regular problem for runners, especially in colder weather if a warm-up routine has not been implemented. Many runners also stretch after the warm-up part of a run, but not all and not everyone is convinced of its value. There is, however, no dispute about the need to stretch after the run.

With the importance of flexibility in mind it is also worth considering attending yoga classes. Yoga is not just about fitness, it is about harmonising body and mind to the rhythm of your breath, but that said it could well improve your flexibility considerably which will help your running. It will also help your mind which, in these stressful times, is always useful.

Massage

Your muscles can also be helped by a good massage every few weeks. This can improve the blood flow and ease tension, which can then make the muscles more efficient. Most physiotherapy clinics will have a masseur or at least will know of a good one locally. You can massage yourself if you know what you are doing, but why not treat yourself to a professional sports massage every six weeks or so; you will feel totally refreshed afterwards!

Follow the plan

This is a recurring theme but you absolutely must stick to your plan. You can look after our body and prevent injury if you keep focused and do not deviate from the schedule that you select. It will ensure that you progress gradually, take part in events when you should and keep speed sessions to a minimum. Ignore your plan and there could be trouble ahead.

Use the gym

Runners always used to think of the gym as a place for those who weren't serious about their running and were more concerned about how they looked than their fitness level. Things have changed and now a huge percentage of those training for their first marathon will incorporate a lot of gym work into their programme. This should include resistance work – of the right type of course – and a programme of exercises based on your core. This is now a focus of many gym instructors. A strong abdomen leads to a good posture and improved stature and if you get this right your running will benefit significantly. Your inner core is a key component of pilates, a discipline which builds strength from the inside out. Pilates has seen a massive growth in popularity in the last three or four years and most good gyms will offer regular sessions. Don't dismiss it as an irrelevance to your running before you have tried it; you may be surprised. Whatever you do, make sure that you embark on a programme put together for you by a qualified instructor and stress that you are training for a marathon.

Find a good physiotherapist

As your training progresses injuries of one degree or other are very common and to make sure that these are dealt with as quickly as possible and with the right professional input it is important that you find yourself a good physiotherapist. There will be many in your local area but check their qualifications and how long they have been practising. There are some very good physiotherapists and some not so good, and you do not want your injury to be treated by one of the latter. Sessions are charged by the hour or half hour and it is generally money well spent. Even when they are injury free, many runners will visit a physio every month or so just for a check up to make sure everything is as it should be.

What to expect when you first start running

Depending on your running experience it is very likely, when you start running, that you will develop sore muscles which will cause you some irritation. This is generally nothing to worry about and is almost to be expected. Your muscle fibres could be subject to very tiny tears, causing swelling. The pain can often be worse on the second day after exercise as this is when the swelling peaks. The most common aches and pains will be in the knees, hips, calves, shins and potentially the Achilles tendon. Expect some discomfort from these and other areas in the early days, especially if you are a total beginner or if you are switching from another form of exercise.

Blisters

One of the biggest irritations in your running career could be blisters. Although not everyone gets them a good number certainly do and all of us are looking for the best way to deal with them! It is particularly an issue in the early stages of your programme as your skin will not be very tough, and they may continue to annoy as you increase your distances. Formed by the skin rubbing against your sock, the build-up of fluid worsens as you run until it eventually bursts. When this happens the exposed skin area can be extremely painful and if not treated the whole process can begin again until blister forms on blister, which is most definitely not a good experience.

As well as being an irritation in training, blisters are a real problem during events and are a real threat on marathon day. You tend to sweat more during a marathon and also pour water over yourself to keep cool. This fluid runs down your body and into your socks. Blisters are then potentially only a few minutes away, especially with your increased pace causing even more friction than normal.

So, can you prevent them? In a word yes, but nothing is guaranteed. Here's how.

- **Keep moisture to a minimum** – Try and wipe sweat away so it doesn't drip into your shoes, and when pouring water over your head lean you head forward and keep the water away from your body.

- **Your shoe choice is crucial** – As discussed previously, shoe choice is crucial for many reasons, none more so than to prevent blisters. The fit is also critical. They should not be too tight or too loose as either could lead to friction and then the inevitable blister. New shoes should be broken in slowly and not on long runs. The design of some shoes can be a problem for some runners and not for others. Some shoes pinch toes more than others, have a higher arch or have a higher heel tab. Seek assistance from an expert and ask the right questions.

- **Choose the right socks** – As important as your shoe choice is the right sock selection. There is a huge number of socks now available on the market, with some specifically designed to prevent blisters. Generally they are made with two layers of fabric that rub against each other rather than your skin, so preventing blisters. They are well worth a try. Cotton socks are the worst option. Again, take advice from a specialist running store. As with your shoes do not wear brand new or nearly new socks for events. Make sure that you have a number of pairs on the go at any one time and use ones with plenty of miles in them on race day.

- **Visit a podiatrist** – There are a number of theories about treating your feet to prevent blisters, such as applying talcum powder or drying agents like methylated spirits, but for the latest advice from a specialist it is worth a half-hour session with a professional podiatrist. A £30 investment could give you many, many hours of blister-free running.

The treatment for your blisters will differ considerably depending on their location and their severity. If they are bad a visit to the podiatrist is essential, especially if they are in danger of becoming infected. If they are fairly small and in an area where they will not become worse it is best to leave them alone, but if the opposite applies then it is best to lance them. This must be done with a sterile needle, from the side, leaving the top untouched. This will help the healing process. Make sure that your hands are clean. Once pierced you should apply an antiseptic dressing to the blister and change it regularly.

Dealing with injury

Do not be downhearted if you sustain an injury or pick up an illness during your training. Time away from your running will be frustrating but it is often nature's way of forcing you to take a prolonged rest. You may experience problems with your knees, hips, shins, calves and many other parts of your body but in the vast majority of cases you will fully recover and be no worse for your experience. Expect that it might happen but do everything possible to prevent it – so many runners' injuries could have been prevented.

Even though you will be frustrated, you must rest and you must seek a professional opinion. You can visit your local GP but this is not always the best option. Many GPs have no knowledge of running injuries and often no interest, regarding them as self-inflicted and therefore a nuisance. Visit a sports injury specialist and preferably one who runs or used to run and therefore can really understand your problems. Make sure that you take their advice. There is little point in consulting them if you don't. So if they say rest, then rest and if they give you exercises to do, then do them!

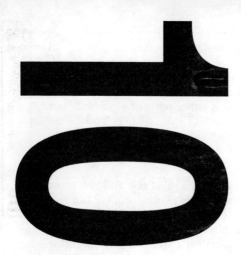

10

fundraising

In this chapter you will learn:
- how to get a charity entry
- how to raise funds
- how to hit your target.

Tip at the top
Start your fundraising early and make sure you have someone to help you in your fundraising efforts.

Running for charity

'Running for charity' is an expression that did not figure in marathon running until fairly recently. There is still a degree of confusion as to what exactly it means, but each year more and more people are doing it, particularly in events like the Flora London Marathon. The London Marathon's race director, David Bedford, developed a guaranteed charity entry programme that has ensured that 'running for charity' is a key element of any over-subscribed running event, whatever its size. But what is it?

In the Flora London Marathon charities have the opportunity to purchase guaranteed entries that they can then pass to runners for an agreed amount of fundraising support – often £1500 to £2000. It's a win-win situation for every one, including the charity which can make a significant mark-up on the cost of the entry if it is marketed correctly. The scheme has proved so successful, however, that there is now a huge waiting list and new charities have to wait many years for entries. Recently another wave of places has become available to open up the opportunity to as many charities as possible, but it is clear that those charities that made the early commitment will reap the rewards for years to come.

In years past it was much easier for the runner to secure one of these charity entries than it is now. While you should be able to secure a place if you're quick enough it may not be with the charity of choice, which may in turn affect your ability to raise the monies needed to fund the place. The charities who know what they're doing can attract many hundreds of enquires each year and as a result can choose their runners after phone interviews and/or internal ballots.

If you are lucky enough to secure one of these guaranteed entries, what next? In some cases the charity will ask you for a deposit which will then be taken off your fundraising target. Not all of them do this, but more and more are as a way of guaranteeing a degree of return. There are still many hundreds of unscrupulous runners who every year remit no money at all or a small amount well under the targeted amount. Not only does this mean that the charity has lost money on that entry but it means that were denied potentially more from another runner who was denied a place. These non-remitters, as they are known, go to great lengths to avoid paying, including changing their mobile phone numbers so they cannot be traced. There is a black list of these runners at the London Marathon head office so if someone does it once they will not get away with it a second time. The deposits that are asked for range from £100 to £300 and they give the charity a degree of security that is essential for cash flow and forward planning of budgets. Once you have agreed to the terms of the place then the charity has only a limited time to replace you should you be unable to carry on training for whatever reason.

At the end of January charities will need to submit their list of runners who have a guaranteed place to the London Marathon office. They then have another month to make any changes. From the end of February no further changes can be made and if you pull out of the race after this date then the charity will not be able to replace you. Although the charity can carry the entry over to the following year, the entry will make them no money in the current financial year. This can have major implications, especially for small charities with only a handful of these guaranteed entries.

Once you have signed up and understood your commitment it is time to set about planning how you are going to raise the £1500 or so which you have agreed to. Obviously you will already have thought about this to a degree before you agreed to it, as £1500 is a lot of money and you need to be confident that you can do it before making any sort of commitment to the charity concerned.

Unless you have some very, very rich friends, family or business colleagues you will find that the fundraising can be as challenging as the training. Many runners admit that the latter was actually easier than the former. However, with a bit of initiative and plenty of determination all things are possible and many runners surprise themselves with the amount that they are actually able to raise. In many cases amounts of £3000–£4000 are remitted, which for a charity is the perfect result.

It's not only those runners who have a guaranteed entry from a charity to whom the phrase 'running for charity' applies; it can be anyone. 'Own-place runners' are those who are lucky enough to get an entry through the ballot system and therefore have not cost the charity the price of the place. If these runners raise funds by running for their chosen charity then minimum levels of fundraising do not apply. If you raise £200 or £2000 it will be very gratefully received. There are some costs involved in looking after an own-place runner, such as the running vest and general administration, but these costs are much lower than those associated with guaranteed-place runners. The more own-place runners a charity can attract the happier they will be.

Raising money for charity

So, just how do you go about raising money for your charity in your next marathon, whether it's your first or twenty-first?

Start now!

It is important that you do not delay once you have secured your entry, whether it is a guaranteed charity place or your own. If you need to fundraise you must give yourself time. Start immediately and not only will you give yourself time but you will also generate momentum which is so vital, especially in the early stages. The longer you leave it the more difficult it becomes and the less inclined you will be to carry on fundraising. This is especially true if you have your own place as there is very little pressure to do it at all in many cases. The sooner you get some money in the bank for the charity, the more likely you are to raise a decent sum.

The timing is also important because it is directly linked to the time that you will be spending on your training. In the first few weeks training time will be low, which gives you more time to fundraise. As the weeks pass so you have to spend more time training and therefore less is available for fundraising, unless you can conjure up some extra hours from somewhere! Assuming that you have ten hours a week available for training and fundraising, as time goes on the bias towards training becomes very significant and you could find your fundraising target looking very daunting if you didn't start early.

Enlist someone to help

Recruiting a 'campaign manager' can make all the difference! Mothers and fathers can be a major help, but it could be anyone who is prepared to assist you in reaching your target. Training for a marathon is not easy at the best of times but raising £1500 at the same time can be especially taxing. Having someone to assist you with the fundraising will make all the difference and could even help you exceed the amount you are trying to raise.

The roles of your 'campaign manager' can be many and varied, but one of the main areas of fundraising is sponsorship and this is where they can come into their own. Online giving, explored below, is a very important part of sponsorship but so is getting good old-fashioned sponsor forms into as many locations as possible. How many places could you get forms into if you had support? Probably a lot more than if you were trying to do it on your own. If you can place forms into ten shops, clubs, bars, gyms and anywhere else to which you have a link, and receive £50 a form, that's £500 straightaway. Your campaign manager will take the lead in getting these forms to the right places and checking up regularly that they are being used and not just tucked away under the counter! More jobs for your campaign manager/support team are detailed below.

Go online

Sponsorship forms are great and have been the mainstay of charity fundraising for years, but a new development is making life much easier. Online giving has revolutionized charity giving in the last few years and with a number of different companies offering the service there is no reason not to get involved. It's easy to get started. All you need to do is contact your charity, find out which provider they use and get the appropriate web address. Then just follow the easy-to-use instructions on how to set up a page and in minutes you will have our own online giving area that your friends, family and work colleagues can access at any time. How will they find out about it? Easy, just send them an email containing the web address of your page with an explanation and hopefully the contributions will come flooding in! It really is as easy as that and again the earlier you do this the more time you will have to let people know about it. This is potentially another job for your campaign manager and support team. Ask them to email the web page address to as many people as possible and make sure that people understand the personal reasons why you are running for that particular charity. Work on the numbers game – the more people who see your web page the more people are likely to sponsor you.

Gift aid

UK taxpayers can help the charities even further by adding their address to your sponsor form or online page. If this information is given then the charity will receive an extra 28 per cent, which can make a real difference to their work. You won't be able to count this towards the amount you have agreed to raise for your Flora London Marathon place but it will help the charity a great deal. All your sponsor needs to do is add their address to the sponsor forms; when you submit your forms the charity will calculate the amount they can reclaim from the Inland Revenue and will deal with the reclamation process themselves. With online giving it works slightly differently. The bigger operators will do the calculations on behalf of the charities and pass the additional 28 per cent directly to them.

Company support

Many businesses offer their employees support for their fundraising efforts. In many instances companies will match the amount that their staff raise, in some cases it is half and in some rare cases it can be as much as double. If you are trying to raise upwards of £1500 this can be an absolute godsend. In effect you only have to raise £750 and with matched funding support from your company you have the full £1500.

There will, however, be conditions with many of these company schemes so make sure you are totally clear before relying on this support. Make sure that you know the upper limit of the fund, any charities that are excluded and the exact percentage awarded. What are the timescales of the fund – do you have to submit an application by a certain time and how many applications will the fund support at any one time? These are all questions that you must find answers to.

How best to collect your sponsorship money

Online giving has changed the face of sponsorship in the last few years and as a result it has made the collection of sponsorship monies much easier. It is likely that however much you do online a component of your fundraising will be offline using sponsor forms, so how do you collect that money?

Chances are you will be dealing with both cash and cheques, which if you aren't on top of your admin can cause a bit of a headache. It is always best to get the money in as soon as you can from your sponsors, preferably well before the race, and when you do send it straight to the charity. There are a number of ways you can do this. One is to find out the relevant charity bank account and pay it directly into that account and another is to pay it into your account and write a cheque to the charity for the exact amount. If your sponsor wants to pay by cheque then encourage them to make the cheque out to the charity and send a batch of them off as soon as you can. The charity will be more than happy to receive your sponsor money as early as you can get it to them both for cash-flow reasons and to show that you are on track with your fundraising. They will give you regular updates and most will send you a letter of acknowledgement every time you submit funds.

Whatever way that you do it, make sure that you get the money in as early as possible. Chasing sponsors after the race will prove far harder than your training ever was!

How to reach your fundraising target

For some runners reaching their £1500 target for a charity place in the Flora London Marathon is reasonably straightforward, but for most it definitely isn't. For the majority it will be a serious challenge and one that will occupy as much, or potentially more, time than the training itself.

Fundraising isn't just about getting sponsors to support you, there are other ways and this is where a good campaign manager is so important.

Talk to the local media

With all the local radio stations, newspapers and websites that have sprung up recently there is now even more opportunity to get some media coverage and this is good for potential fundraising. The more you can expose people to your name and the name of your cause the more chance you have of attracting sponsors. It is, however, important that you give the media a hook, something to really pin the story on. Don't just say you are raising funds for a particular charity. Say why you are running and what it will mean to the charity. What personal element will make all of the difference when a journalist is weighing up whether to use one story over another? Why will your story get coverage while another may not?

Remember that the closer you get to your event the more people will be vying for coverage, so make contact as early as you can – but only when you have a good story to tell. You won't be on your own either. Many charities have a media department that will be able to help you get local coverage. They often have media release template forms that you can use; simply 'fill in the gaps' and send off the form to your local media and it could be the start of a sustainable media campaign. You can, of course, put together your own media releases but why try and reinvent the wheel when your charity has already invented it for you?

Don't give up in your attempts to get media coverage. If it doesn't work the first time then try again with a different tack. Think carefully about the approach you take; don't just bombard media with releases. It's easy for journalists to bin releases and much more demanding to read them. Encourage journalists to read yours by making them interesting. It will all be worth it if your story receives great coverage and you secure many extra sponsors as a result.

Seek help from local businesses

Wherever you are in the world it is very likely that there will be local businesses nearby, many of which understand that they have a moral responsibility to support charities, and supporting runners in their marathon fundraising attempts is a great way of doing this. Be selective and approach businesses in the same way that would the media. Give them a real reason why they should support you. Some will have adopted charities, so find out who they support and you may find one that supports the charity that you are running for.

Talk to businesses about how you can get involved. Don't just expect them to send you a big cheque; you will need to work for it. Why not suggest that you go along after the event with your medal and talk to the staff about your experiences and how their money has helped the charity? Outline where the charity is planning to spend the funds. Suggest that you include the company logo on your running vest and sponsor forms, both online and offline and try and mention them when dealing with the media. The more exposure that you can give the company the more likely they are to support you. Giving support to charities is one thing but if it is linked to increased business then that is another.

Involve your local pub or club

If you are a regular at a local bar or club then get them involved. Hopefully you won't be visiting as much as you used to, but here's a chance to say, 'I'm off to the pub', and not be told off!

Pubs and clubs are often happy to support regulars in a challenge such as running a marathon and this will often be critical in helping runners meet their target. Their involvement can range from allowing you to use a collection tin to a pub quiz that they may even organize on your behalf. If you don't ask, you don't get, so have a chat with the landlord when you next see him and chat through some suggestions. Remember as well that others may ask the same thing, so get in as early as you can.

Party time

You may not feel comfortable with the idea of asking guests for a donation to attend a party, but at times like these you may well have to do things that are a little different. Think about organizing a party either at your home or an external venue and charge an entrance fee which more than covers the cost. Any profit then goes to the charity. It could be at your local pub or at a hotel nearby that may do you a deal on the room and catering. You might be surprised at the response of those you ask. They may well be more comfortable with the idea than you are! Most of us want to contribute to charity and if all we have to do is attend a party then that makes life very easy. This also applies to dinner parties that you may already host. Ask guests to make a contribution to your cause.

Hold a raffle

Raffles may not be the latest fashion but they are a good, reliable way of raising funds. See if you can get hold of a decent prize – potentially donated by a local business – and a book of raffle tickets and away you go. There are obviously rules and regulations that need to be closely adhered to if you really want to take this seriously, but if it is just for friends, family and colleagues then the more basic approach will be fine. Even if you raise £100 it takes you another £100 closer to your target. The better the prize the more you are likely to raise, so spend some time getting something that people will actually want! Last year's Christmas presents probably won't cut it!

Jackpot-style competitions

There are many different types of competitions you can run, but one of the most popular is the 'guess my finishing time' type. Simply produce a chart with a range of finishing times on and a space next to each in which you can write the name of the person who has chosen that time. The person who chooses the time nearest your actual finish time on race day wins the jackpot. You decide how much it costs to enter and you decide the jackpot. This can often be half of the money received with the other half going to charity. This may sound very simple, but often the quickest and easiest ways to raise funds are. Keep it simple for you and your supporters and the charity will reap the rewards.

Initially, raising £1500 for a guaranteed charity place in an event like the Flora London Marathon can seem extremely daunting but it doesn't need to be. Plan properly, get started early and enlist someone to work closely with you, be imaginative and you may well find that you end up with a lot more. Remember also that if you have your own place already any contribution that you can make will be greatly appreciated.

11

the week before the race

Tip at the top

The last few days before a race can be frustrating. Make sure you try and relax and do not overdo your last few runs. Patience is the key now.

The week before the race is a very strange one and very different from all the other weeks in your marathon training programme. In terms of the amount of running that you need to do it's more like one of your early weeks as the pressure to run is off and looking after your health becomes the number one priority. If there is any week in your programme when you should wrap yourself in cotton wool then this is it. Welcome to taper week!

One of the over-riding feelings during this week is one of frustration. You feel at a loose end. You want to run but you really shouldn't do too much. For the first time in your life you can really imagine how the caged big cats at your local zoo feel: capable of much, but only able to do a little.

Many people's marathon training can come badly unstuck during this week for two principal reasons. Firstly there are those who are in a state of panic. They know that they haven't done enough and rather than take it easy for the last week or so they decide that this is the perfect opportunity to make up for lost time, especially if they have missed a week through injury or illness. Wrong. It is absolutely the worst time to be increasing your training. If you haven't prepared properly by now then it is far too late to cram in extra miles. You are far better trying to get by on the day with what you've already done – as long as you've done at least enough to finish – than try and do extra in the vain hope of bettering your finish time by ten minutes. It is quite likely that your body will not recover from this week of cramming and your performance on race day will be severely hampered by the late mileage. Even worse you could pick up an injury. If you really haven't done enough training even to finish then the best advice is to leave the event you're planning to run and pick another. If you have a place in London you can defer for a year and this is definitely the best option.

Second, there are those who just can't stop training. If you have followed your training plan, chances are you will be in the best shape of your life. You will be feeling invincible and the idea of running very little for a week will not be one you relish. You will continue to go about your life that week as normal and run consistently, thinking incorrectly that some extra speed sessions are just what you need to fine-tune your body for the big day. Wrong again. This group of people are, in the same way as the first group, in danger of damaging everything that have they worked hard for over the previous few months. You must follow every aspect of your training programme, including this last week, which is one of the most important. Not only that, but you must also make compromises during the week that may prove difficult. You will feel frustrated and probably a little bit irritable, but it will be worth it. Remember that it's only a few days and you deserve a rest after the hard work that you have put it in.

How much should I run?

The answer, irrespective of the training plan you are following, should be very little. Your body has been worked extremely hard and it needs time to recover before it is put through its ultimate challenge. Whatever you feel like, you must not exceed the time suggested on your plan or you will affect your race day performance.

This week, and indeed the whole of the taper period (see Chapter 05 for more details), which is around two weeks, is a critical time as it gives you the chance to fuel your body for the 26.2 miles to come. It is a very long way and you must give yourself the best chance of walking away from the finish line believing that you did your best. You will feel extremely disappointed if you look back and think that you never fully recovered from that extra, unscheduled long run in race week.

The most effective race week running programme is one that focuses on minimizing damage to your body. You must look after yourself, which is why the gym is often the ideal environment for the last few days. Use the treadmill and do two or three light sessions of half an hour or less. Walk if you prefer not to run. The idea of these runs is to keep the muscles warm and ready for action on the big day. None of these miles will affect your performance on the day – unless as mentioned, you do too many – they are in the plan to make sure that you keep your muscles active and don't stiffen up. Don't change your running style or slow the treadmill down too much as this could potentially cause an injury. If you would rather do these last few runs outside don't try any new routes, stick with what you know.

What about other exercise?

The same rules apply to other exercise that apply to the amount and type of running that you should do. You must do nothing to excess and try nothing new. It is fine to substitute some other forms of exercise for running in this final week, but not if you are looking to increase the time spent exercising. Brief walking is a good idea, as is cycling, but as ever, be careful.

If you want to lock yourself away safely in the gym, you could use the stationary bike, rowing machine, stepper or other CV equipment, but only if you are used to them. Don't decide to take up the indoor rower the week before your first marathon. If you do it could be a recipe for disaster.

As with the running, take it easy and do nothing too strenuous. Don't set yourself any targets and do not put yourself under any pressure. This week is all about saving yourself for the big day.

Is any event preparation needed?

The answer to this question very much depends on the race that you are entering. If it is one of the big marathons like London or New York then you will have to attend the pre-event exhibition and collect your number and timing chip. This will inevitably mean that you have to plan this into your week, especially if you live out of town. Generally speaking these exhibitions, or expos, are three or four days long and are held a few miles from the start of the race. They can at first sight appear very daunting and if the nerves are going to surface then it will be here, especially when you first walk into the building and see the shear scale of it all!

The expos are often held in huge exhibition halls and can have upward of 100 exhibitors, all encouraging you to purchase their products or enter competitions. So, not only do you first have to pick up your number, you then have to negotiate your way through a myriad of running-related products and services, the majority of which will seem very appealing. However, this is again where you have to exercise some caution. Anyone who has been to a big exhibition will know how exhausting they can be and those linked to the big marathons are no different. Don't spend hours wandering around as it will do your legs no favours. If you do want to see everything and it will be useful if you do, then take your time and take regular breaks. This is especially important if you visit the day before the race. It's not such an issue if you're there on the first day as you will have plenty of time to recover. You will feel pretty disappointed if your race day performance is affected by spending too much time on your feet at the expo.

Event expos are always busier on the Saturday than at any other time, so you should always try and attend as early in the week as you can. If it opens on Wednesday then try and get there on the Wednesday. There will, of course, be logistical reasons why you can't get there earlier if you live many miles away but if you are fairly local then it will be well worth the effort to go sooner rather than later. On occasions the organizers may allow another runner to collect your number on your behalf, but don't count on it. If they do then you will need to sign the appropriate form and they will need to take relevant identification.

One of the biggest temptations that you'll face at a big running expo is to buy new kit which you end up wearing on race day. Buying kit is a good idea as there are some great brands available, many at decent prices. You can always rely on an expo for a deal, especially as the show progresses and the exhibitors want to get rid of stock. However, buy it and pack it away. Do not be tempted to wear it on the big day or you will suffer. This applies to shoes, shorts, tops; anything that could rub. You should only wear kit that you are familiar with and never be tempted to try anything that is not well worn in.

What should I eat?

Running a marathon requires a huge amount of energy and much of this energy is derived from food groups that are consumed during this last week. It is vital that you eat correctly and do not stray from the good habits that you will hopefully have picked up over the previous few months.

As you would expect, the most important food type is carbohydrates. By now you probably never want to see another plate of pasta again in your life, but in race week it is important that you make one last effort! Don't forget that eating carbohydrates isn't just about pasta. Potatoes and rice are excellent alternatives for this vital energy fuel, so if you really can't stomach any more pasta then these two will be fine.

Whatever you do, make sure that you do not try anything new. Even with your pasta make sure that you try no new sauces. Stick to tried and tested options that you know will not cause you any problems. Trialling new options now is an extremely bad idea. This also applies to snacks, running-related products like energy bars or gels and drinks. You must stick to what you know or you could have a reaction that will put paid to your race day aspirations.

Of major concern to many runners, particularly first-time marathon runners, is what to eat the night before the event. The same rules apply. Never try anything new and stick to familiar options. This is often easier said then done but it is never more important than in the few hours before the race. This is the time you want to avoid stomach problems at all costs. A creamy pasta sauce rather than a plain tomato sauce would be the wrong choice if you are used to the latter. Go with what you know and make sure that you make every effort to go to a restaurant that suits your needs. On one occasion I had a Chinese meal as my pre-event nutrition and nice as it was I suffered the consequences from mile one right through to the point two of the 26.2 miles! The last time I had eaten Chinese was more than six months previously and as this was the only restaurant within a mile of my hotel I thought it would be the best option. For the next marathon I spent time during the day sourcing a more appropriate option.

Your pre-race meal should also be eaten early rather then late to ensure adequate digestion takes place. You do not want to be running a marathon with the previous night's pasta still undigested. The earlier you eat – 5–6 p.m. being the best option – the better. Before you hit the start line you need to ensure that you have visited the toilet and, without sounding too crass, have emptied your system as best you can.

Although the previous night's meal will be key to the success of your race day experience, your intake in the three or four hours leading up to the start will also play a role. More often than not you will have to get up many hours beforehand and even though food might be the last thing on your mind you will need to take on some sustenance. One of the best options is tea and toast about three hours beforehand with bananas and cereal bars excellent alternatives. The same rules of familiarity apply though. None of these suggestions should be new to you – even the jam on your toast if you have some. Depending on the length of your journey to the start and the time you have to hang around beforehand, take some food with you and always pack some water. You must make sure that you begin your race well hydrated, although guard against drinking too much water, a litre in the two hours leading up to the start will be ample.

How do I deal with the nerves?

If you don't get nervous before a marathon, especially the first one, then there is something wrong. Nerves are an integral part of marathon running and for the first-timer they are with you pretty much from the time you enter the event to the minute you run over the finish line. It is in race week, however, that they are at their most extreme and especially at the expo.

Nerves are generally an issue because of a fear of the unknown, and they will reduce as your familiarity increases. This is very much the case with the marathon. How will I get to the start? Will I know where to line up? Have I done enough training? Will I be last? How will I know where to go? These are all common questions for a first-time marathon runner and all totally understandable. As you do more events, so you will have fewer questions. Nerves are in time replaced by an adrenaline rush, although the feeling is often very similar.

So, how do you deal with nerves? Ultimately, whatever you try and do to alleviate them you will still get nerves and that is not a bad thing. However, you can reduce them, which is important for you and for those around you!

Try and talk to people who have run your chosen event before and ask for some tips about getting to the start and about the course, to put your mind at rest. Don't necessarily ask them for training tips though as too much input in that area can cause confusion, particularly if they are not qualified.

Read as much as you can about your event, both in the race-day instructions that you should be sent a month or so beforehand and on the race website. These days event websites are incredibly comprehensive and contain everything you need to ease all your fears. It is worth visiting your race site many times to get a flavour of where you will be running.

Train well! Many runners experience real problems with nerves simply because they have not trained sufficiently and they are concerned about the implications. Poor preparation will lead to an unenjoyable race experience and there is little you can do to alleviate these nerves apart from train properly. Follow your training plan and this type of nervous problem won't be an issue for you.

What about my sleep pattern?

You may well find that your sleep pattern changes during your marathon training, an issue that is linked to the problem of extreme nerves. For many people this is one of the most significant personal challenges that they have undertaken and inevitably they will dream about it – or have nightmares!

From the early days after the entry is confirmed, right through the training up until the night before the event it is very common to have restless nights thinking about the big day. You may experience the full range of emotions from dreaming about winning to having nightmares about coming last. Rest assured that this is common and it is nothing to worry about. There will be many occasions when you have trained so hard that you are almost too tired to sleep, with aching muscles preventing you from enjoying the hours of slumber that you may be used to.

There is unfortunately no real cure for these problems apart from ensuring that you go to bed earlier than you might be used to in an attempt to recover some of the hours that you may lose. There will be many cases when, after a long run, you can't keep your eyes open so rather than fight it, go to bed and try and recover with some decent sleep.

You will need to accept fairly early on that your sleep pattern might change – it doesn't always – and you will need to make up the shortfall whenever you can. Also try not to have too many huge nights out during your training as this will exacerbate the problem.

Is it worth having a massage?

During your training it is well worth having a regular massage as it relaxes the muscles and can identify any problem areas that may need further attention. There is no better time to have a massage, however, than the week before the race. With the nerves and tension that you will inevitably be feeling you will need relaxing and there is no better way of chilling than an hour on the masseur's table. Don't go for a general massage – it needs to be a deep sports massage where the muscles are worked hard rather than simply soothed. You will feel like a new person when it's finished and raring to go!

Should I run if I don't feel well?

If you feel unwell at any stage during the last week you may well have to make a very difficult decision and defer your entry until the following year. In the Flora London Marathon you are able to carry over your place (subject to repaying the entry fee), although if you're running in a charity place it is up to the charity if you are able to run the next year as they own the place.

Ultimately the most important issue to consider is your health. Running a marathon is a huge challenge at the best of times and is never to be taken lightly. Running when you are not feeling at your best is unwise and potentially can be very dangerous. Your heart will be put under even more pressure and major problems could result. However hard the decision not to run may be there is always next year. Each year hundreds of runners start a marathon when they should not and in the majority of cases the experience will not be the same as it would have been if they had been at their best. Think carefully and do the right thing.

12

the big day itself

In this chapter you will learn:
- what to do the night before
- what to do on race morning
- how to develop a race plan
- how to enjoy your big day!

After months of training this is what it is all about. The big day has arrived and today is the day you will be physically challenged as never before. If you've trained well you will have absolutely nothing to worry about. Yes it will probably hurt, but if you have followed a plan it will be one of the most memorable days of your life. If you haven't trained well it will certainly be a memorable day, but for very different reasons.

What you get out of your big day very much depends on what you have put into it. This also includes the last few hours beforehand and during the event itself. You can have a textbook preparation period and then ruin it all by making mistakes in the last 24 hours that can change a potentially great day into an awful one. Don't lose focus and make sure that you stick to your game plan. Nerves can often get the better of you at this stage but don't let them upset your big moment!

The night before

Sleep is an important issue and you must get plenty of it during race week. Chances are you won't get into the deepest sleep the night before the event with thoughts of the day being uppermost in your mind. You might be having dreams or nightmares, but whatever aspect of the race you're thinking about your sleep will no doubt be affected. Bearing this in mind, it is essential that you make sure that you sleep well on the Thursday and Friday of race week. Get plenty of sleep in reserve beforehand and you will feel much better on race day if you miss out the night before!

Choosing your hotel

If you have to stay away from home the night before the race make sure that you choose your accommodation carefully.

Don't jump at the first thing that comes along even if you are leaving it until the last minute. If you end up on a busy street with constant traffic in a busy city then you may have some sleep issues that will ruin your race day experience.

When you've settled on the place that you're going to stay, make sure that you tell them you're running a marathon, you will be in bed early and you need the quietest room in the building! You may find a decent hotel only to find that one of the wings overlooks a public space or the air conditioning units. Get it right and you will benefit but if you get it wrong your race could be ruined.

Kit preparation

Don't leave any of your preparation until the morning of the event. Do everything you need to do the night before. Lay out your kit, attach your number to your vest and attach the timing chip if there is one, to your shoe. Make sure that the number is fully visible and the safety pins that you use to attach it do not rub against your nipples. There is nothing more painful! If a timing chip is involved, read the instructions fully before you tie it to your shoe. There will be a diagram with the instructions so make sure you look at it.

Make sure you have all your medical supplies with you and packed in the kit bag that you will take to the start. Vaseline is an essential so do not leave it at home.

Check that you have your other clothes laid out in your room ready to wear in the morning. In most parts of the world it will be cold on race morning so you will need to wear some extra gear to the start. Normally there are large baggage buses positioned in the start area that will drive to the finish if it is a point-to-point course (like London or New York) or remain in place if it is a loop course (like Chicago). This is where you leave the gear that you aren't running in and pick it up when you finish. Some races, like London, give you a specific kit bag that you must use. If you hand any other bag to the staff manning the baggage buses they will not take it. This is something else that you must check before the morning of the race. Have you got your bag to hand?

It is also a good idea to take some old clothes or a bin liner to the start that you can wear once you have handed in your kit bag. You will still have plenty of time before the gun goes and you will need to stay warm. When the gun goes you will need to remove the old gear or bin liner and leave it on the side of the road.

These are not the sort of things that you should be checking on race morning. You must have everything ready for when you wake up for one of the most important sporting days of your life. Panic about a missing piece of gear is the last thing you need in the hours before you start running.

And don't forget your running watch.

Set at least two alarms

At this stage of your preparation it is essential that you leave nothing to chance. Do not under any circumstances leave anything to anyone else. You have come this far and you should not allow anyone else the opportunity to upset what you have worked so hard for. This applies as much to race day as any other day and potentially more so. It is a good idea to arrange an early morning call through your accommodation if they have the facility, but do not rely on it. Set the alarm on your phone and take a travel clock with you as well. Many runners have missed their event because they didn't receive wake up calls as promised and I know this from experience! Do not leave it to others to get you up, do it yourself. Set your alarms yourself and check them twice. Most marathons will require you to get up very early. For a 9 a.m. start you need to be there just before 8 a.m. and even with a short journey this means getting up around 6.30 a.m. The further you are from the start the earlier you will need to get up and the smaller the margin for error. If you are looking to do the ING New York City Marathon buses leave Manhattan around 6 a.m. and in some events in countries with hot climates the race itself can start at 5 a.m.!

Race-morning nourishment

Remember to give yourself plenty of time before the start to have something to eat and drink. It shouldn't be much but you must allow yourself to digest it fully before you start your run. Again you should not have anything that you aren't used to and nothing too complicated. Tea and toast is usually pretty safe as are bananas and muesli bars, but again only a brand that you've had before. If you don't want a hot drink then stick to water. Don't be tempted to eat too much. A full cooked breakfast is not a good idea, so however much you might feel like it try and avoid one at all costs. Keep it light and remember that the energy stores you will be relying on during the race will come from the food that you consumed the day before. If you get that intake correct your performance will be much better for it. Throughout the final few hours before the race you need to start hydrating yourself but do not drink too much. A litre will be enough to make sure that you start with plenty of water in your system.

Take water and some snacks with you to the start line in case you get hungry while you wait for the race to get going, but don't eat because you're bored. Again, only eat foods that you are used to. You can't go wrong with bananas at this stage.

Getting there

Long before the eve of the event you must work out exactly how you are going to make your way to the start. All of the big races will send you extensive guidance on the best way there, but will only be of use if you read it properly. You will receive plenty of information from the organizers in the days beforehand and you absolutely must make sure that you absorb it all. Getting to the start of the major marathons can be very different. In Chicago the start is right outside the main city-centre hotels so it can be a five-minute walk for many runners, whereas in New York organizers lay on buses to take 35,000 runners over to Staten Island. In London the start is in Greenwich Park, which involves public transport for most people. Extra trains are provided to get the runners from the centre of London to the park and the times of these trains will be clearly outlined in the pre-race pack.

Read it all and then read it all again. As well as the overground mainline trains the underground network is also running and will be used by thousands of runners who can link to the Docklands Light Railway to complete the journey to Greenwich.

As you can imagine, the earlier you leave the less crowded the trains will be and the less stressed and harassed you will be on arrival. You can then relax in the park, warm up properly and enjoy the unique atmosphere. The longer you leave it the worse it gets. There is nothing worse than arriving at the start area under pressure. Ideally you need to be at the start, whatever marathon it is, about one to one and a half hours before the official start time. It may end up being more than that in some cases, such as New York, because the situation dictates it, but it should not be there any later than that. You need time to prepare both mentally and physically and this timescale gives you that time.

It is always far better to have time on your hands at the start than to arrive late. Work on the assumption that there will be a problem on the trains and build in time accordingly. Assume that a train may be so full that you can't get on it and you may have to wait for the next one. If you are driving to the start of a race (not recommended for one of the majors) assume there will be heavy congestion and nowhere to park. Then, if there is a delay you will be prepared for it.

The final hour

This is probably the most stressful hour of your whole marathon preparation. You are so close to getting underway but still a very, very long way from the finish. Everyone around you will be nervous and you will all just want to get going. What should you do now?

Try and maintain your composure and make sure that your nerves do not get the better of you. This is easy to say and a lot harder to do, but you must try your best to stay in control.

Ensure that you have emptied your bladder and bowel. It's a good idea to take toilet paper with you to the start just in case none is available. It normally is but don't count on it. There will be plenty of portable toilets in the start area but inevitably they will get very busy the closer you get to the start time. Don't leave it too late or you could still be in the queue when the gun goes off. It is important that you are well hydrated, but don't drink too much in the final hour or you could be looking for the next toilet all the way round the course.

Within 45 minutes or so before the start you will need to deposit your kit bag in the appropriate baggage bus. Make sure that you go to the bus that corresponds with your race number. In most big races you will have received a sticker for the bag which matches your race number. Make sure that you stick this on correctly. With your bag deposited you must keep warm using the old throwaway gear or bin liner that you should have taken with you.

Before heading to your correct starting area you must warm up gently and do some light stretches. Don't do too much and don't engage in unfamiliar stretches just because someone near you is doing them. Stick to what you know and what you do before your long runs. It is quite easy to get injured even at this late stage and there can be nothing more frustrating.

In all of the big marathons you will be allocated a starting 'pen' according to your expected finishing time. You will have indicated this on your entry form. You must make your way to this pen, which will be very clearly marked, well before the start of the race. Bringing 35,000 people together in one place is never easy and there has to be a system which everyone sticks to. Don't move into another pen and don't leave it too late before you take your place. At the start of the Flora London Marathon most runners will be in their pen around 20 to 30 minutes before the start.

This is a time when you will be especially nervous. There is now nothing more that you can do but wait. All the preparation is done. Look around and enjoy this unique moment. Chat to fellow runners and enjoy these few moments of real camaraderie. Everyone is in this together.

When finally the gun does go off in one of the majors, like London, it is likely that there will be no movement whatsoever! There are so many people involved that if you are towards the back it could take you around 20 minutes just to get to the start line. This is a strange time. You know the clock is ticking but you just have to be patient and wait your turn. Don't be concerned about times though. Your timing chip will only be activated once you hit the start line and not when the starting gun is fired. However, the clocks throughout the course will record the time from when the gun was fired.

Before you get to the start line, or whenever the gun goes, whichever you are most comfortable with, remove the old gear or bin liner that you have been using to keep warm and discard it to the side of the course, trying not to trip anyone up in the process. It is a spectacular site watching thousands of people getting rid of the warm gear at the same time. Charities will collect it once you have gone and you can rest assured that it all goes to a good home.

Once you hit the start line don't assume that you will be able to get into your stride. You will still need to be patient. It will take a considerable amount of time to be able to the run at your target pace. Many people start in the wrong pens and it takes a while for it to all settle down.

Setting a race goal

It is always good to have an idea of your potential finish time but you should not become overly concerned by it. It is very normal for you to take far longer than your anticipated time as you may have based it on your longest run. This may have been 20 miles and you have assumed the last six miles will be run at the same pace. They won't be. The last six miles will be significantly slower unless you have trained exceptionally well and run a steady race with plenty in reserve. That is very unusual so if you are setting yourself a target make sure you take into account that the last few miles will be much slower than the first.

The more you worry about your time the less you will enjoy the event. Unless you are a top runner and looking to improve your personal best don't worry about the clock. Of course you want to do well, but it's more important on your marathon debut to enjoy it and come back for another. If you want to set a target make sure that it is a realistic one that you can hit. Don't fall into the trap of overestimating your potential time and chasing an impossible target all race. Give yourself a chance!

The race itself

It is vitally important that you have a race plan in your mind before you start and that you stick to it. Do not under any circumstances be influenced by anyone you see around you either at the start or during the race. You must stick to your plan and not deviate unless there are extreme circumstances.

The start

At the start of the event you should go off slowly. Do not try and keep up with people around you because you think you look fitter than they do. Many people struggle to lose weight so just because a larger person than you is ahead of you does not mean that you should try and overtake them. They may well be in better shape than you but just not look it. Go at the pace you have trained at. Starting slowly will help you conserve energy and help you in the latter stages. If you go off too quickly you could literally run out of energy and have nothing left for the challenging final few miles.

During your long runs you will have settled into a pace that you will be able to maintain during the marathon. If you deviate from this on race day you could well struggle. Keep it constant and don't be drawn into quick bursts of speed by the crowd or runners around you. While it is fairly easy to keep to a constant speed in training on isolated country roads it is a totally different issue when you are being cheered on by hundreds of thousands of people and with other runners everywhere you look. The crowd will encourage you to engage in 'high fives' and there will be regular cheers and anthems that you can get drawn into. While you want to soak up as much of the atmosphere as you can and contribute to it wherever possible you also need to keep your energy expenditure to a minimum, so be careful and don't get too carried away.

The early stages of your first marathon will all be a bit of a blur. You have trained so hard for this and here you are running along with thousands of others, your senses overpowered by the sights and sounds of a truly overwhelming occasion. It is quite likely that your race plan will be neglected and you will run far too fast. You need to be very aware of this and ensure that you do not get sucked into all the excitement. Remain in control. It is hard to describe the atmosphere at a major event like the Flora London Marathon or the ING New York City Marathon and absolutely nothing will prepare you for it. All you can do is accept that it is going to be out of this world and make sure that your running in the early stages is not adversely affected.

After a few miles most runners will have settled into their pace and the need for constant overtaking or being overtaken will ease. There will always be plenty of movement as some people tire sooner than others, but generally speaking after about six miles the field will be much more stable. By this stage you will find it much easier to run at your normal pace and the distractions, although many and varied, will have become a little bit more familiar. The atmosphere will still be incredible, the pubs will still have bands playing and the crowd will still be cheering relentlessly, but now you will have had time to absorb it all and you can focus on your running.

Timing and pace

If you don't use a running watch or have forgotten it don't worry because at each mile marker at big city-centre events there will be official race clocks. The time, however, will be the time that relates to when the gun went off, not when you crossed the line. It's a good guide though and lets you know how long each mile is taking. Keep your eye on these clocks or your watch through each mile without getting too obsessed. Try to keep a steady pace as much as you can and be as consistent as possible. Do not mix up your pace too much and remember in the early stages that you have a lot of hard work ahead.

As you approach the half-way point you must ensure that you are not running the same pace as you would for a normal half marathon. You should be much slower. At the end of a half marathon you should feel like you don't have a lot of energy left, you should have pushed yourself to the finish. At the half-way point of a marathon you should have plenty left. The second half will be much tougher and you need to provide for it. The exhilaration and excitement of the first hour or so will potentially take its toll but you must not let it.

Mind over matter

As you enter the second half of the race your mind will start playing tricks on you. From here on in it is a case of mind over matter. You will be fighting battles with your mind non-stop until the finish and you must be prepared for this. If you have trained correctly and you have done plenty of long runs this will be familiar and you will have a degree of experience. If you haven't then this will be new territory. It is almost as if you have two voices in your head: one will be telling you to stop and have a break and the other will be telling you to carry on. Don't listen to the negative voice, especially as you head towards the worst part of the course between miles 16 and 18. If you are forced to walk then you must do so, but try and do so as fast as you can. Some runners adopt a walk/run strategy from the outset but for most the walking only starts when they cannot physically run anymore. Try not to walk for too long if you can avoid it as you could be on your feet for far longer than you had planned.

At this point your mood will be at its darkest and your morale at its lowest. You must dig deep and pull yourself through. Inevitably if you haven't trained hard enough these feelings will be intensified. Welcome to 'the wall'. Hitting the wall is an expression of folklore proportions. It is the sensation that marathon runners experience when they literally run out of energy. By now you will have been on your feet for over three hours and for many runners much longer, and you will feel as if you can't go on. Your glycogen energy stores will be seriously depleted and if you have trained insufficiently this is when it will really show. Its impact can be minimized by eating plenty of carbohydrates beforehand and following a decent training plan. If you do these things correctly you may never hit the wall and you will wonder what the fuss is all about.

The last few miles

If you're running one of the majors like London or New York the crowds will be huge during the last few miles and they will play a critical role in helping you get to the finish. As you struggle past the 20-mile mark you enter new territory. Most beginner training plans do not require you to run more than 20 or 21 miles on your longest run, so as you head past that distance you will be on new ground. Mind games will challenge you further and you will wonder if you can cope. This is where the crowd come in. They will urge you forward and you will find inspiration from their enthusiasm. Throughout the race you will be ticking off the miles in your head and no more so than the last few. As you move through into the early twenties you will find new energy reserves and then suddenly you only have two or three miles left.

It is then that you really know you are going to finish. You will suddenly find fresh legs and you will thoroughly enjoy the race. The crowd will continue to lift you and you will now begin to feel incredible emotions. Many first-time runners will shed tears at this stage, especially as they enter the last mile or so. The event now begins to become a blur. It is similar to the start where the sights and sounds almost sweep you off your feet. There is nothing like it. You cannot train for the last few minutes of a major. As you train you should visualize this part of the race. Images of running past Buckingham Palace in London or through Central Park in New York will keep you going during the darkest, wettest and coldest nights of any training programme. All of us need inspiration during training and there is nothing more inspiring than this stage in your first big race. Absolutely nothing.

As you cross the finish line your dream will have been fulfilled and you can enjoy your moment of triumph. Make sure that you try and take in the enormity of it all.

Food and drink

During your training you will have learnt how to take on water and you will have trained with the energy drink that will be available during the marathon that you have chosen. At least, you should have done.

Getting your food and drink intake correct is one of the keys to a successful marathon. There are no magical formulas but there are guidelines that you must follow. You should drink at every water station and you must not drink too much. How much is too much? The right amount is a few sips every mile. You must never wait until you are thirsty before you drink. By then you are probably already dehydrated. Then you have problems. Water stations in the majors can stretch over 200 or 300 metres so avoid the crush and keep running towards the back of the station where it will be far less crowded and collect your water there. It will probably be in a bottle with the cap already removed, although it could also be in cups which can be quite difficult to master. Take a few sips and throw the bottle or cup to the side, making sure that you do not trip another runner up in the process. Keep drinking like this throughout the marathon. Small amounts should be taken at every opportunity. Some runners carry the bottles with them between stations almost as a type of 'comfort blanket'. This is fine as long as only a few more sips are taken, but do not drink the full bottle.

Every big event will have an energy drink available at the aid stations, although not as often as the water. Generally it will be available every five miles or so and it can feel like a life saver as the miles pass. You must, however, train with the exact brand that is made available at the specific race that you have entered. In London, for example, it is Lucozade Sport orange pouches and you must train with this exact product, not a similar one but this exact one. This is not a ploy to increase sales – it is simply that each drink is made up of subtley different components and to an untrained stomach they can have unsettling effects! The more you train with it the more your stomach will adapt to it. Whatever race you run make sure you find out the specific brand and stick with it for a few weeks beforehand. Whenever you take the energy drink on offer dilute it with water. This will reduce its potential impact on your stomach but still give you the same energy boost.

Energy gels are another very useful energy source on which many runners rely, especially in the latter stages. These are generally not available on race day, so you have to take them with you. You can purchase belts to which you can attach the sachets, although you should practise running like this – it isn't to everyone's taste. Gels are concentrated carbohydrate which must be diluted with water. They can have a real impact on your energy levels and help prevent you hitting the wall. Aim to take about four or five during a marathon and no more. If you take more than this the impact on your stomach could be devastating.

At many marathons members of the crowd may offer you sweets or fruit along the course. Although there are times when these seem too good to turn down you must be extremely cautious, particularly if the food is unwrapped. You just do not know what you are eating and if for some reason you get a reaction your race could be over. Be sensible and make the right decision. If it's a boiled sweet, which can really help your energy levels, and it is well wrapped then it is probably okay, but if there is any element of doubt then turn it down.

If you think you may not be able to last four or five hours without eating and that water and energy drinks will not be enough then you must take something with you. Gels, sweets and chocolate bars can all be taken with you in belts. If you think you may fall into this category then buy one and try it out.

Get your food and drink intake right and you will be well on the way to a very memorable day.

The perfect day

There is so much to take in on race day that you are probably wondering if you will be able to cope with it all. The answer is, of course, yes. Your training will ensure that your legs can cope; your race day nutrition plan will ensure that your stomach can cope and your strength of character will make sure that your mind can cope. You will inevitably have a few wobbles on the way around, both mentally and physically, but if you hold it all together then you will have the adventure of a lifetime.

In summary, you must prepare for this day like no other and you must be focused on yourself. This is all about you and as a result you must be single-minded and selfish if that is what it takes. This very much applies to your race strategy. Stick to your race plan and do not be affected by anyone around you. Make sure you try nothing new during the build-up and on the day itself and do not even be tempted to deviate!

Stay focused and you will have a great day out.

13

a real-life experience – Sue Thearle, BBC

In this chapter you will learn:

- that marathon running is for everyone
- that your work and home life can be adjusted to fit the training
- that injuries can hold you back.

The start

I knew I was in trouble when the email arrived in my inbox. It
was from Tim Rogers, an old friend of mine who was now
running a running website (no pun intended). I hadn't spoken to
him for ages, about two years in fact, and yet suddenly out of the
blue I was invited to lunch. But something about this particular
invitation smelt fishy, in fact worse than fishy, I smelt a rat, a big
fat one with huge teeth. It was there in black and white, blinking
provocatively at me: 'I have a challenge for you …' Instinctively
I feared the worst. Nobody ever asks you out to lunch to discuss
an interesting proposition unless they want something,
something big. But what could it be? What could an 37-year-
old, slightly overweight sports presenter with a young child
possibly offer a running guru? Suddenly something clicked
inside my head. Oh my god, he's going to ask me to run the
marathon, the bloody marathon. Oh dear God no. My fingers
hovered over the keyboard. I could turn down the invitation. I
could say I was too busy, which as a working mum with a noisy
little cherub was true. But despite my mild panic attack, I had to
admit something about Tim's missive had struck a nerve. So I hit
reply. 'Love to see you again,' I gushed and promptly slumped
back in my chair and stared disconsolately at my flabby midriff.

I'd known Tim forever – since I was 18, had bad hair (the result
of an ill-advised demi-wave perm) and an even bigger bottom
than the one I currently possess. He's a lovely man and jolly
decent company. The only downside, if you can call it that, is his
obsession with exercise. He's run about a billion marathons
(okay, actually 40 something and counting, including one at the
bloody South Pole) and I always secretly feared that one day he
would try to drag me into his maelstrom of long-distance running.

By the time I called him the next day I actually felt a bit sick.
After about ten minutes of idle chitchat, I sensed that the
moment had arrived to cut to the chase. I asked the question
casually, 'So err, what's this challenge you've got for me?' I
stared into the middle distance and waited …

'Well,' said Tim, 'you know I do a lot of work with charities for my running website. One of them has asked me to help them put together a celebrity team to run the marathon this year.' Oh bugger. 'I mentioned your name and they thought you would be great. So how do you fancy it?' Like a bucket of cold sick actually. 'Come on, you know you can do it.' No I can't. 'Sue, are you still there ... Sue?' My heart had sunk through the bottom of my flared trousers by the time I finally mustered the energy to speak. 'Well first and foremost I don't consider myself a celebrity. And secondly I can't run any further than about two miles. So errrr, NO!' I bellowed in a slightly shrill voice. I had my excuses, pretty decent ones I thought, lined up and ready. 'Tim, I've got a daughter now. She's ten months old and needs me.' Good start Thearle – keep going. 'I also have a job, which involves getting up at 4.30 a.m. at least once a week. I have a husband, a life, friends and two cats called Brucie and Tarby (they are light entertainment pets). How am I possibly going to fit it in – quite apart from the fact that I will not be able to run 26 miles?' Brilliant. That concludes the case for the prosecution. It's in the bag. I felt a bit like Ironside. 'And last but not least,' I added, playing to the gallery, 'I am not built to run marathons.' Mentally I added, 'and I have an arse the size of Norway, hips that were meant to bear children and thighs that will forever be prefaced with the word thunder.'

'Yes you can,' Tim responded immediately . 'I've helped loads of people just like you to run marathons. You already go to the gym and run, which is a massive head start. You just have to build up slowly and keep an eye on your body, but it's so achievable – it really is.'

Oh Christ I'm going to have to argue with him, I thought miserably. Fortunately Tim had a better idea. After explaining that the charity in question was Help the Hospices and giving me a bit of background about the people involved with this particular project, he let me stew in my own juices and we agreed to meet a fortnight later and talk things over.

I was in turmoil. You see, the idea of running a marathon really had crossed my mind before, several times. I really liked the idea of being able to run that far, but genuinely believed I couldn't. I'd always thought that long-distance runners had a different gene, because I just couldn't understand how they could keep going for mile after tedious mile, hour after tedious hour. But I admired these people immeasurably, and secretly yearned to be one of them and that's why Tim's offer really intrigued me. It was an ideal opportunity to get really fit after having a baby.

I was still carrying 12 extra pounds following Holly's arrival and here I had the chance of being coached by a guy who had run over 40 marathons. There wasn't a thing about training he couldn't tell me and I knew he would be a brilliant mentor. I was also soon to turn 38. Not ancient, but not young either and if I was ever going to run the race, then now seemed like a good time. And last, but by no means least, the charity concerned really appealed to me. One of my closest friends spent his last days in a hospice. They are wonderful places full of wonderful people and I wanted to help. Yes, I knew it wouldn't be easy. In fact it would be a nightmare juggling childcare and work and yes it would be difficult physically, but nothing was impossible. I would just have to be incredibly organized and stick to a rigid training schedule.

As I wrestled with my conscience, everywhere I looked all I saw was really attractive people jogging effortlessly along the byways and highways of London. The bounce in their step mocked my lumbering gait and the glint of the sun off their shiny white teeth dazzled me. Not a panting fatty to be seen anywhere. It was really annoying. By the time I actually saw Tim for lunch in mid-September I didn't know my arse from my elbow, which is odd because one is much bigger than the other. But Tim was blissfully ignorant of my turmoil as we talked for the next three hours. His opening gambit, I must say, was brilliant. He told me about a friend of his who had asked him for some training. She was a size 14 smoker who had never run a step in her life. She hated exercise and was only turning to the demon treadmill as a knee-jerk reaction to the break-up of her relationship. Apparently, when she and Tim met for their first training session they didn't run at all. They walked for ten minutes at a brisk pace and she was gasping for breath. Of course the fags had to go, which they did, and suddenly this lady began to enjoy it. They built up to running slowly and methodically. Tiny steps at first and then 15 to 20-minute runs. Soon she was galloping for an hour and had lost a stone in weight. She had entered the Great North Run that October and had already completed another half-marathon. She was also entered for London and had thanked Tim repeatedly for helping to change her life. Christ, now it was like being on a make-over episode of *This Morning*. At the end of this cheery anecdote the chunky chips arrived. Carbs, I joked weakly as I smothered them with tomato ketchup.

Tim turned his attention to me. The idea of fitting all that training into my busy life really worried me. And quite apart from anything else I wasn't sure I could do it. Tim's arguments were compelling. He told me exactly how I could do it all. He had brought along a beginners' training plan for me. It was a 25-week plan so I had loads and loads of time to make up my mind and think about it rationally. I suppose the hardest part for me was making the leap from being the modest runner I was – two miles, two or three times a week in the gym – to suddenly running 26. Tim kept reminding me that the progression was gradual and that it took months to go from fun runner to marathon runner. The key though was that you could do it.

I must confess I was really intrigued now. Because you work in sport, people automatically assume you're good at it and I must admit modestly that I am. I have always been a pretty good football, hockey and tennis player. My sixth-form hockey team were county champions both indoors and outdoors and I played for Millwall Lionesses during a fairly successful football career. I also got to the third round of the Perranporth Grass Court Tennis Championships in 1982 which, let's face it, is a hop and a skip from being British number one. I am also a keen golfer, so eye to ball co-ordination I can do.

Athletics, though, has always been a different matter.

Because I had such a good sporting pedigree, the teachers at school always assumed I would be good at athletics and shoved me into it. Alas, my lack of dazzling speed soon became apparent – 43 seconds for one particularly humiliating 200 m sports day effort where I surpassed myself by falling over at the start. The next step was obviously field events which was even worse. I discovered I had an aptitude for the javelin, which was okay because everyone loved Tessa Sanderson and Fatima Whitbread. But alarmingly I was also quite good at the discus. This wasn't so good. The discus event in the early 1980s was dominated by butch Eastern European women who had taken so many steroids they looked like men – quite large men with facial hair that would make Magnum PI proud. It wasn't an event you really aspired to. So you see, long-distance running had never been a part of my sporting past, something which I had always regretted. I have always associated running with long-limbed, lithe, pony-tailed beauties who float down the track with ne'er a care in the world. This fantasy works quite well for me, until I run any further than about 400 m and go red in the face and generally look like a fat potato.

But these thoughts were banished from my mind as Tim convinced me I could give it a decent go. I pored over the training plan in huge detail. The first few weeks looked okay and I figured that I could get to around week eight or nine without too much bother. The plan really was for complete beginners, aimed at people who really had never run before, so that made me feel very encouraged. But when you looked beyond the first ten weeks, as of course I did immediately, I felt intimidated. I added up some of the longer runs and quickly surmised that workouts of over three hours featured in the schedule. It made me feel faintly nauseous. All the old doubts came flooding back. How could I ever run that far? What was I thinking? This was a stupid idea, it really was, and I almost tore up the papers then and there. But I didn't. I persevered with the thought at least and decided that the best course of action was to have my holiday and mull things over. My plan was to do some running while we were away and see how it went. If it went well, then I would attempt the marathon. If it didn't, I wouldn't. We met my husband Scott's parents there and got into the routine of going out for a run while Holly had her morning nap. It worked perfectly. The seafront at Barmouth is lovely and I must admit I enjoyed myself. Our route was a mile and a quarter in length so there and back suited my two- to three-mile routine. But by the end of the week I got cocky and decided I would attempt a five-mile run with my husband, or Steve Ovett as I like to call him.

He is one of those irritating people who was born to run. His build is perfect for distance running – slim legs and a perfectly formed bum which facilitate a running gait that a gazelle would envy. But he understood how important it was for me to try and do this. In my head I knew that if I could run five miles, it meant I could do the marathon. I wasn't sure how, exactly, or why, but I just felt very strongly that it did. Scott agreed that we would make this attempt the next morning, so I went to bed that night full of doubt and a little anxious. Having backed myself into a corner, I knew that I wouldn't refuse this challenge, but at the same time I was still worried about my lack of running ability. As Scott had rather unkindly but honestly pointed out, I did run very slowly. He could run backwards and keep pace with me. In fact a pensioner looked like he might overtake me at a brisk walk on one of our morning excursions. That is one of the reasons I have always avoided it. But as I approached the nether regions of my 30s, I was beginning to feel that the time had come to try and change.

Friday morning dawned bright and warm, perfect for a gentle run. I got up early with Holly and after breakfast showed her the route that mummy was going to take later that morning. She gurgled appreciatively I think. I can't tell you how many times I tried to back out of it in my head. By 9 a.m. I'd convinced myself I'd slipped a disc, by 9.15, I was sure that my ankle was hurting and by 9.30 I actually felt physically sick. This was the earliest indication of one of the things that I feel lies at the heart of successful running and that is a positive mental attitude. Of course, I did not possess one and that was why I was turning into a hypochondriac. Still having failed miserably to contract an illness serious enough to warrant my withdrawal from this sporting odyssey, my fate was sealed and I found myself strapping on my trainers at the stroke of 10 o'clock and staring miserably out of the window towards the sea. I wanted so much to achieve this target and at the same time I couldn't shake the feeling that I would fail. It wasn't a pleasant sensation. My husband was lovely and seemed to understand my lack of confidence. He distracted me with conversation as we strolled down to the front and before I knew it, I was peering along the promenade ready to go.

Now I realize it's hardly the start line of the 100 m at the Olympics, but to someone like me it seemed like it. The challenge that it represented was just as great in my little world, and while I wasn't going to get a gold medal for finishing a five-mile run, it meant just as much to me. The next hour and a bit was a struggle, but I did it and that was the key. It took me just over an hour and my Achilles was hurting by the end of it, but it was a fairly momentous achievement. I enjoyed the pleasant realization that from a fitness point of view the actual distance I was running was not a problem at all. In fact, I was surprised by how easy I found it. For me the problem was obviously always going to be mental and one that would plague me for the next six months. It's hard to explain the sense of achievement I felt as I jogged towards the end of our little adventure. I remember looking out to sea with a feeling of moderate euphoria as the wind blew sand into my face and I stepped in a huge pile of dog poo. It seems so silly to get so excited about a run along the seafront, but to me it represented so much more. After a little over an hour I knew much more about myself, my body and my capabilities. In short it was a revelation. As I reached the bus stop that marked the end of my epic journey, Scott enveloped me in a huge hug and told me how proud he was. I could have cried tears of joy and relief but I didn't, because I was too busy making a life-changing decision. I was going to attempt the marathon.

Shopping

The first thing I did after deciding to do the marathon, was tell everyone I was going to do it. The psychology behind this was simple. The more people who knew I was doing it, the less chance of me backing out. I felt excited and incredibly nervous about what lay ahead of me and I must admit, I also felt a little bit self-important when I told people of my cunning plan. Their reactions were all incredibly positive. There really is an enormous respect that, quite rightly, surrounds marathon running. You can say 26 miles out loud as many times as you like, but it still has a mythical quality to it. Most people are in awe that you could even attempt such a feat and that is the most common reaction I elicited. The fact that I had a small child as well as a job and demanding cats, meant that a great number of my friends thought I had gone nuts. 'How will you fit the training in?', was the most frequently asked question, along with, 'Have you taken leave of your senses?'

But without fail every single person I told wished me luck. Either they knew I would need it, or they just felt extremely impressed that I was even contemplating it. Either way it made me feel very special, a little but like when I first told people I was pregnant. In fact it's quite similar in a way. You get carried along on this wave of euphoria without really knowing what awaits you. Women who've had children smile benignly and refuse to meet your eye when you ask them how painful labour is. People who have run marathons nod sagely when you tell them that you are going to do one. Then when you ask them how hard it is, their only reply is, 'It's a long way.'

It was the verbal equivalent of the Masonic slight of hand, given by a group of people who know exactly what the experience is really like, but don't want to put you off by telling you the truth. Now that I am a member of both the marathon and mother clubs, I shall be doing exactly the same when anyone asks me about either in future.

Deciding to undertake the challenge did feel like a weight being lifted off my shoulders and it was all worth it just to hear Tim's reaction when I phoned him to tell him that I would be doing the race. He whooped with excitement when I broke the news and then started talking gibberish at me. I later realized that he was in fact talking shop, running shop that is and I don't mean a retail outlet. He was straight into the nitty gritty of training, which I don't mind telling you, took a little of the gloss off it for me.

I wanted to bask in the glory of just saying I was going to do it for a little longer. The thought of actually running was something I could quite happily put off. But Tim was having none of it. We arranged for our first training run together (joy), which was to take place the following week. In the meantime my instructions were to get out there and get running as quickly as possible.

As 'running' and the word 'quickly' have never been present in the same sentence where I am concerned, I ignored Tim's advice and decided to go shopping instead. Now, while I admit that I may appear a little bit shallow at this point, in mitigation I would like to point out that if you are going to take any sport remotely seriously, there really is no point unless you have the right gear. The fact that shopping is one of life's finest pastimes in my opinion is just a happy coincidence. And let's face it girls, a running legging can make or break a pair of thighs and I had to look the part. I was now officially in training and I had to make sure that nothing was left to chance. Tim had also very sensibly advised me to get some new running shoes asap, because he felt the trainers I had were contributing to my aching Achilles. He instructed me to pay a visit to the London Marathon Store to get some gear and so that was my next port of call.

Scott sighed in a resigned fashion when I told him I would be heading there to buy all of my kit. He knew that I would return armed with every possible gismo including, he suspected, a satellite navigation system to track my every move, albeit very slowly. He was however mistaken in that assumption. I didn't buy one. What he didn't realize was that the only reason I didn't get one was because I got to the till and discovered I had already spent close to £300 and that was with a discount.

The first thing you notice about the Marathon Store is the ticker above the door. It tells you down to the second how long it is until the big race. When I went, there were still 180 days to go. As I stood mesmerized by the second countdown, it occurred to me how far away it all seemed, not just in the length of time but the whole concept. It was still a little difficult to envisage me bouncing down The Mall at the end of 26.2 miles.

Tim had instructed me to ask for Gary and he was an absolute doll. He listened very patiently as I rambled on about being a hopeless runner who had been talked into the madness that is the marathon. He had run it a couple of times so I had tons of questions which he tried to answer, but when I pressed him on what it really took to get round, all I remember him doing is nodding sagely, telling me it was a long way and then pointing me in the direction of shoes. See, I told you they all do it. We started shopping in the shoe section. The beauty of the right shoe means that running does feel a lot easier. I can say that now with hundreds of miles on the clock and a marathon under my belt, but it is the one thing I would recommend to everyone above all else. Gary whisked me down to the basement where there was a running machine and a foot-scanner and he got me to run across the scanner so he could see exactly how I planted my foot. Different shoes offer different kinds of support, depending on your running gait, and I apparently needed a medium support shoe. I had gone to the shop straight after a *Breakfast* shift and must have cut a slightly bizarre figure running over the scanner time and time again in full make-up and a suit. Gary was too much of a gentleman to say anything, but I did occasionally catch him staring at me in a quizzical fashion.

I tried on a selection of items and gave a couple of pairs a test drive on the running machine. I made a vain attempt to look cool as the minutes ticked by and my face reddened, which was no mean feat under three layers of thick foundation. I plodded along pluckily with Gary peering at my feet and asking periodically whether I was okay. When he finally gave me the okay to step off, a bead of sweat had miraculously muscled its way onto my top lip. We had, it turned out, identified the perfect running shoe for me, but to be honest I would have plumped for a pair of flip flops at that point.

Having recovered my oxygen levels, I headed upstairs to the clothes section to inspect the running tights. Now the larger lady like my good self needs a running tight that is a little kinder on the lower body and I tried to disguise my substantial thighs with a patterned pair which were essentially black. I also plumped inexplicably for a pair of grey three-quarter length pants. As an experienced shopper I have learnt the hard way how to disguise my curves rather than accentuate them, so I avoid pastel trousers at all costs. So quite why I decided that grey skin-tight lycra would be a sensible choice, I shall honestly never know. Suffice to say the grey pair have been worn once before being discarded at the back of a drawer, which means they are a heartbeat away from the charity shop.

I also picked out three running tops, a decent bra and lots of pairs of socks as I fell into the trap of imagining myself as the lithe pony-tailed beauty I had always aspired to be. I hadn't been paying any attention to what I'd been picking up price-wise, but I came back down to earth with a bump when the till started to make whirring noises and steam came out of the top. I had been so busy chatting and asking tons of sensible questions, that I had taken absolutely no notice of the cost. I could feel myself going pale beneath my make-up, which was no mean feat. I think Gary detected the colour change as well, because he very kindly offered me a small discount. I think he felt sorry for me on so many levels at that point, that he felt compelled to make it all better. But even with a discount, I had still managed to blow the best part of £300 and although I had certainly got more than enough to get me started, I instinctively knew that the grey pants weren't right and that I would inevitably be back to buy even more. Financially it was a depressing thought. I gulped and paid. But to this day I look upon it as the soundest investment I could have made. You need to feel comfortable if you are going to be running hundreds of training miles and the right shoes and gear are essential.

So I was ready to embark on the journey of a lifetime and for me the toughest part was knowing that my destiny lay in my own hands. I was the only person who could make this happen. I was in control of my body, my training, my diet, my whole preparation. If I didn't do this, there would be no-one else to blame but myself and this was a kind of pressure I had never experienced before. There was nowhere to hide. This might sound strange coming from a woman who went through 27 hours of labour to produce my beautiful daughter, but having a baby and doing the marathon are two completely different things. Your body takes over when you are pregnant and in labour. Yes, there are things you can do to help the process along, but essentially your body is biologically designed to do it. With marathons, you're not necessarily built to run them. However, you are in control of what you do and how you do it. Do the training and look after yourself and you will complete the race, unless you get an unlucky injury. Fail to prepare and you must prepare to fail. Oh dear, this was going to be very hard indeed.

Running

My doctor is a lovely man called Quentin and we chatted enthusiastically about the marathon as he examined my

Achilles carefully. He is also a keen runner. I know this because I almost knocked him down one evening when he ran across the road in front of my car. Fortunately it was one of those rare occasions when I was wearing a hat, so he didn't recognize me. I, of course, have never brought it up and I do hope he isn't reading this now. I quizzed Quentin on his running pedigree. Like a lot of people I talked to, he'd done a half marathon and felt that 13 miles was more than enough for him. But he was genuinely excited about my plan to do the full monty and this, my friends, is one of the best things about marathon running. Everyone thinks you're fantastic, because you are. So many people just shook their heads in quiet admiration when I blurted out that the marathon was my next big challenge. The truth is that relatively few people have the courage to try it, and when you meet someone who does, well I think they deserve a bit of a fuss. And that was exactly what my doctor thought as well, because he spent ages marvelling at my ambition. I suppose he appreciated how hard it would be juggling a child, a job and training, but his words of kind encouragement really touched me and gave me even more determination, if any were required, to finish what I'd started.

When the adulation had finally finished and I had stopped daydreaming about an OBE for my fundraising efforts and general goodwill to strangers, I was brought back to earth with a slight bump. The doc confirmed that he had indeed detected some localized swelling and recommended I see a physio as soon as possible. I was referred to a practice close to where I live, which was perfect, and with more pre-training felicitations ringing in my ears I strode confidently out of his office. I felt a bit foolish because I didn't have a dramatic limp, or a limb hanging loosely at my side. Instead I had a small, pesky lump on my tendon which didn't really bother me at all until I started to run, when it quickly became extremely painful. I like to have tangible proof of physical discomfort, a bruise, an ugly scar, something that means any sympathy can be well and truly justified. But some airy, fairy explanation about a sore Achilles with little obvious evidence of a war wound did make me feel like a bit of a fraud. But I reminded myself that I was in fact a tip top professional athlete now and just because crutches weren't required, it didn't mean that I wasn't critically injured. So, armed with a letter of referral and a perky smile, I marched to the physio with some optimism. I was hoping I would be running again in a couple of weeks. Little did I know I wouldn't be running another step for two months.

The first physio I saw was called Steve. He was from Melbourne with a marvellous Aussie accent and an outdoor glow that everyone from that part of the world seems to possess. Inevitably he had run three or four marathons before in phenomenally fast times and had loads of advice on what to eat, drink and take by way of supplements while I was training. I was really getting into marathon talk in quite a big way now, because I wanted to know everything about other peoples' experiences. I was fascinated by the different approaches to training. Some people told me their longest run before the race was 15 miles, others had done 22; there was so much variation it intrigued me how preparations could be so different, yet end up producing the same result. I had become a piece of blotting paper, absorbing every valuable nugget of information and making copious notes if anything struck me as especially suitable for me. Although I had the training plan for beginners, my intention was to construct my own regime based on a combination of that and my own lifestyle. Everyone has different needs and circumstances. In my case I had a small child, a job, a flexible nanny and a lovely husband who all contributed massively in allowing me to train. You do really need a reliable support network if you have kids, people who can step into the breach for an hour or two to allow you to do the running. Jan, who looks after Holly when I work, and of course the delightful Scott, were exceptionally good to me and allowed me the flexibility to get out and run when I needed to, but then I did brief them both with military precision about what I wanted to do and when I had to do it. When Scott was at home I would go out when Holly had a lunchtime sleep, so I wouldn't miss any of her awake time. That wasn't always possible, but by and large it meant I could plan my runs at certain times on designated days and that is crucial. You have to have a system. You need to know what you're doing and when you're going to do it, because without it, you will quickly lose interest and give up. Let's face it, there are too may distractions, especially when your training coincides with the height of winter. The weather is rubbish and the last thing you really want to do on a cold January afternoon is go out running, especially if Ben Hur is on telly again. However, if you know that's the only chance you'll get for two days and you appreciate that you have to do the miles or else you won't be able to run a marathon, then a system will work for you, I promise.

Steve's immediate diagnosis wasn't too bad. I had a thickening of the ligament around the tendon which would need a combination of rest and treatment. That was the good news. The bad news was he couldn't tell me how long it would take to heal. It was one of those irritating injuries that required great care and attention, because if I tried to rush back too quickly, it would flare up and keep me out of action for weeks again. This was less encouraging, because I really wanted to know when I could run again. Having decided to go for it and take on this momentous challenge, I wanted to throw myself into the training programme immediately. But I couldn't and it was an almighty pain in the arse.

Steve assured me that if I did all the right things, I would recover fully and be more than capable of completing the training and the marathon itself. But he did warn me that half the battle with the marathon is actually getting to the start line. He had seen hundreds of patients whose dreams had gone up in a puff of smoke because they had trained too much when they were carrying strains and minor muscle aggravations. Those small injuries had turned into honking great big ones which had meant they never made it to the start line. As I listened to this my worry gland kicked into action immediately. After years of avoiding distance running like the plague, I suddenly wanted more than anything to do lots of it now, but my mind and body weren't singing from the same song sheet. The key though, I've discovered from bitter experience, is to stop running when something hurts and get it sorted. Simple but brilliant advice. Steve reassured me that I was in good enough shape to do it, I just needed to listen to my body. So I decided to take his advice. I made myself at home, plumped up two huge pillows on the treatment table, and lolled into a comfortable position for my first ultrasound treatment. As he treated me, Steve told me an absolute horror story about a female client who had trained in a textbook fashion to do the London Marathon. She was on course to run something between three and a half and four hours, which is lightning quick in my book, but her race came to an abrupt end when someone caught her heel as she ran around the Cutty Sark. She fell flat on her face, broke her nose and was rushed to hospital in an ambulance. I listened in stunned silence. Life can be such a bitch sometimes. I made a mental note: no-one is coming anywhere near me on race day. I don't care if there are 35,000 people there, no-one's going to touch me or my feet.

So that was how I spent the first of many happy trips to my local clinic. A combination of ultrasound treatment and vigorous massages meant I was a weekly visitor, where I got to know

Steve and another Steve very well. Liverpudlian Steve, to give him his correct moniker, was also as fit as a flea and had run a half marathon. Kayaking, though, was his big love and that was where he was now devoting his athletic efforts. He and Aussie Steve kept my spirits up as November drifted aimlessly by and the Christmas decorations started to go up. Still there was no sign of me being anywhere near able to run again and I was beginning to get a tad annoyed. Every time I went into the office, or saw any of my friends, they all asked immediately how the training was going. Because I made such a hoohah of announcing my marathon intentions, everyone quite rightly wanted an update. So I felt a total loser when I had to admit I hadn't run a step. I explained that my Achilles had been troubling me for some time and unfortunately was a little more problematic than first thought. As usual everyone was charming and supportive, but it was deeply frustrating. I've always been rubbish at waiting for sports injuries to heal. In fact I've often blithely ignored medical advice and played football and hockey when I knew I really shouldn't have. This time it was different though: I was older, a little fatter, and something inside me just knew I couldn't ignore the advice I'd been given, because if I did, I had a funny feeling I'd be watching the race again rather than running in it.

But at least it wasn't all bad. Okay I couldn't run, but I was able to try and maintain some kind of fitness at the gym. Swimming and cycling were allowed and to stop me feeling as if I would turn into a sumo wrestler without any exercise at all, I did try and do something a couple of times a week. It wasn't the same. I never feel like I've truly worked out until I stagger off the running machine with my face an attractive colour puce, looking as if I need medical attention. However, any port in a storm and cycling, occasional stepping and swimming was better than nothing.

I was still having physio at least once a week, sometimes twice, and one night in late November I popped in for my regular appointment only to discover that both Steves were unavailable. Having got to know them both so well, I was a little irritated that neither was there and that I would have to go through my tedious injury history with someone new. But the lovely Liam (from Cardiff – honestly it's like the League of Nations in there) assuaged my fears with his charming bedside manner and within about five minutes I had gone from slightly aggravated client to agreeing that acupuncture might indeed be the way forward.

Now I don't know about you, but I have always been a teeny, weenie bit sceptical about things like that. I think that Ying and Yang are great names for giant pandas, but not something that adequately describes my state of emotional being. And I'm sorry, but feng shui sounds like a fungal rash. Whenever I've heard anyone talking about acupuncture, I have listened politely while feeling just a teeny bit superior. But here I was, gushing effusively about the benefits of alternative medicine and agreeing enthusiastically that my meridians were indeed out of kilter. Liam showed me where the pressure points in my calf were and explained that the reason why they hurt, which they did actually very much, was because all was not well with my back. The two Steves had also identified this as part of the problem with my Achilles, because problems with my spine were causing me to overcompensate physically and manifesting themselves in the left leg, specifically my Achilles.

So when Liam suggested acupuncture I tamely agreed. It suddenly seemed like a great idea, because frankly nothing else was working. I was bored with sitting on my backside and doing nothing and I would have agreed to anything at that point just to get the process moving again. So there I was, Mrs Cynical, lying face down on the treatment table, having needles flicked into my back, murmuring gently that it really wasn't painful at all. In fact it wasn't. Liam warned me it might make me feel a bit sleepy at which point I reverted to type and scoffed. How Liam must have laughed when he came to remove the needles 20 minutes later, to find me snoring gently and dribbling attractively out of the corner of my mouth. There was also a big towel mark on my face.

As I did my best to pretend that I hadn't actually been asleep, I didn't notice at first that the pressure points in my leg felt totally different. But they did. There was no pain at all. It was as if the needles had sucked the pain away. Now I've just read that back and it sounds dreadful, but that's the best way to describe the drastic change in discomfort level. When he'd pressed and pushed the point in my calf at the start of the session it had felt like a bruised bone. Now there was nothing. Indeed he could have sat on my leg at that point and still I would have felt nothing. I was officially a convert. In fact I was so chilled, I was mentally contemplating putting braids in my hair, turning vegetarian and buying a 2CV.

I was roused from my daydream by a gentle shaking of my shoulder. I had nodded off again. Great. Now it looked like I had narcolepsy to go with my bad Achilles. But happily the drowsiness was short-lived. I went home and raved about the benefits of acupuncture as Scott fixed me with an unblinking stare. But even he was partially convinced as I snored happily in bed that night, one of the best night's sleep I have ever had. And no, before you jump to any conclusions, I am not being paid by the British Acupuncture Society or anything like that. I can only speak as I find and for me acupuncture was a delight.

My next visit to the physio proved the point. My Achilles was suddenly starting to co-operate. The thickening of the ligament had subsided somewhat and we could now finally begin to think about me doing some exercise. Hurrah. At last a breakthrough. It was the end of November and the clock really was ticking now. I hadn't done any running for seven weeks and I couldn't wait to get going. Steve (Aussie Steve) told me to wait two more weeks. He wanted to be absolutely sure I was ready. All the long hours spent on the treatment had been worth it. I was about to start running again.

The training

So I finally and officially started my marathon training on 15 December 2004. It was only a gentle run – a one to two mile jog to re-introduce me to the joys of running. It was of course further than my physio had advised me to go, but I was so keen to get some exercise and see if I could still put one foot in front of the other. Well apparently I could and it was to be the start of a gruelling few months. My routine was fairly simple. I ran four times a week, on a Sunday, Tuesday, Wednesday and Friday. I had adapted the training plan to fit my lifestyle. Not everyone has the time to run five times a week, as my training plan suggested, so I was trying to do the same amount of work in four days. It was the only way I could do all the running and work and most importantly see my daughter and spend time with her. It wasn't ideal, but it was the best I could do. I was quietly confident about my plan because it felt achievable and also because I was so mentally focused on what I was doing. This for me was only ever going to be a one-off experience. I was sure I hadn't discovered a new hobby late in life. I wasn't suddenly going to spend the next ten years running marathons all over the world. No, I just wanted to do one marathon in my life and London 2005 was it. It meant I would have to dedicate myself to training for the next four months of my life, but that's not a huge chunk out of your life and I was sure it would be worth it. My plan was to add a mile to my longest run every week, so the first Sunday I did five miles for my longest run and the following Sunday I did a 10 km run. I also tinkered with my other runs to try and gently increase the mileage, but there were a couple of weeks when I just sustained the same level of running to give my body a chance to get used to all the running I was doing. I'm not going to pretend to you that it's easy, because it's not. There were times when I wanted to scream, burn my running shoes and kill Tim for persuading me that this was a good idea. But the thing that kept me going was finishing what I'd started. I had to find out if I could make my body do this. It fascinated me to the point of obsession. That, coupled with a huge amount of sponsorship and the potential embarrassment of failing in front of millions of people was strangely somehow enough to keep me going.

Another essential part of training is making sure you don't get bored. You must vary your runs or you will end up wanting to jump into the river I used to run up and down on cold winter afternoons. For some variation I used to drive around various parts of South West London just to gauge the mileage and know how far various routes were. That meant I could do a combination of road running, park running and gym work and again that kept me mentally fresh and helped my knees. Psychologically I had another fantastic reason not to back out, because the *Breakfast* TV audience knew I was doing it. The programme were keen to monitor my progress and had decided that I should do a video diary every couple of weeks updating everyone on my progress. The programme also thought it would be fun for me to have a running mate, so they could follow both of us as we built up to the big day. I was swamped with hundreds of emails when I first advertised for a training partner. I couldn't believe the response. There were so many heartbreaking stories of people running for mums, dads, sons, daughters, nephews and nieces, who either had incurable diseases or had tragically died. So many of the emails reduced me to tears it was impossible to choose. In the end we plumped for a lady called Heather from Bedfordshire who had beaten breast cancer. She had two grown-up children and was aiming to do around the same time as me (five hours ish).

So that was my life, running, talking about running, doing more running, doing some filming of me running and then, oh, doing even more running. My programme definitely worked for me because I didn't miss one session through 'can't be bothered-ness'. Although there were many times when I didn't want to go, I always went out. I missed one week of training on doctor's orders with a throat infection, but other than that I stuck to the schedule and started to run further and further each week. Tim had told me I had to be up to over 30 miles a week by the time the end of March arrived, so that is what I aimed for.

The first big hurdle for me was to run the adidas Silverstone Half-Marathon. Unfortunately, I had been suffering from a throat problem for the previous three weeks, which culminated in a trip to the doctor and the prescription of a steroidal spray to stop a river of mucus running down from my nose into my throat. Then things became worse from there – and the less said about the race itself, the better! I did complete the half-marathon, though, which was my goal. I simply wanted to raise money for my charity and get a marathon medal – so finishing was all that mattered, rather than the time that I did it in.

The final chapter

So April arrived and with it the joy of the taper. I didn't realize that you started to cut down your training as the big race approached, but you do and the best bit about it is that suddenly 12 miles will seem like a casual stroll. In terms of my longest run before the race I did 18 miles the week after my 16-mile race and it was fine. By then my body had become so used to running long distances, I must confess I quite enjoyed it. Like so many runners, I find the first couple of miles are the worst. Once I get past that stage of arguing with myself about whether I should be doing it at all, I really get into it. A lot of people go further than that for their longest run, some not as far. Again it all depends on personal taste, although my opinion, for what it's worth, is that you should really aim for at least 18. Do the maths on that one because on race day you still have another eight and a bit to go ... marathon's are a long way you know.

The week before race day you pick up your race stuff and register at the expo in Docklands. I went on the first day to try and beat the crowds, which I think I managed, but incredibly some people leave it to the last minute and are banging on the doors to be let in when it closes on Saturday evening. That is way too late, so my advice is, as with most things to do with the marathon, leave plenty of time. Don't miss the big day because you forgot to get there sooner. You can get your name printed on your vest there, which I did and it was one of the best decisions I made. Everyone cheers you on and that can be a massive lift on race day.

After the administrative stuff was done I just sat and waited for race day. It felt weird not running as much as I had and there is a temptation to sneak out and try to do more miles, but you don't need to. They are all in the bank waiting to be cashed in and you need the rest, you really do. The other thing I really concentrated in during the whole training programme was what I ate. Pasta, water, pasta, water is a great mantra the week before and indeed all the way through. Make sure you eat plenty of carbohydrates because they do give you an extra spring in your step.

And so to the London Marathon 2005. I got up at the crack of dawn to make sure I was there on time. I had no intention of missing the biggest sporting day of my life because of London Transport and believe me some people do. I had packed my race-day bag about three weeks before, and meticulously planned my journey, so I knew exactly what time I would get there to do some filming for BBC *Breakfast* before the race. I had done all the other things you should do, like wear my race-day outfit on my longest run to make sure it didn't rub, pack my number carefully in my bag and panic wildly for the 48 hours prior to the race. So I was all set and raring to go. The train journey to south-east London passed without incident, although I sat opposite two giant Cornish pasties, who I instinctively knew would pass me during the race. They did, along with the Wombles, Rupert the Bear, two giant speakers and a ten-man centipede.

The atmosphere on Blackheath was one of the most incredible things I have ever experienced. There are thousands of people milling around, all smiling nervously and rubbing Ralgex furiously into various body parts. The hottest attraction though are the toilets and it is worth getting there early just to suffer a half hour wait for the bog, but needs must unless of course you are Paula Radcliffe. Even though I was there an hour and a half before the off the morning still flew by and suddenly I was saying an emotional farewell to my long-suffering husband and dashing off to dump my bag, have a wee and get to the start. I barely had enough time to do all that but I didn't have time to worry about it as I jogged to the start line and shuffled off on the biggest adventure of my life.

I still find it hard talking about the marathon without crying because it was such an emotional experience for me. The battle with myself and my lack of running esteem was bad enough just to get to the start line, but the battle I had with myself on race day was titanic. The first few miles were fantastic. I felt great, found a good rhythm, kept out of trouble and just pottered around the course. The crowds are enormous and everyone is screaming at you. All the kids on the route want to high five you, which I had been warned about, because it is very easy to get carried away in the euphoria of the moment and exhaust yourself by about ten miles. So I didn't get too carried away, I just concentrated on what I was doing and set my first target, which was nine miles, where my husband and group of about 16 friends and family were waiting for me.

It was a boiling hot day, as it can be in April, which threw me somewhat after all those subzero training runs. I was wearing my vest and a long-sleeved shirt which was too much, but I knew I could change out of it if I was too hot, when I saw my husband. On reflection that was a silly risk, I should just have opted for the vest, because you do warm up very quickly, but I got away with it. Everything went fine until the six-mile mark when my Achilles started to hurt. It hadn't bothered me at all really, so its return was not something I had not anticipated. But I had decided that nothing was going to stop me completing 26 miles and even if I had to walk most of them, I would. That was my pre-race strategy – get round at all costs. If you have to walk some of it, that's okay – finishing is the main thing.

I met hubby and co at nine miles and took off my top, slapped on the factor 25 and generally larked about. I took loads of photos and spent a good five to ten minutes chatting. Big mistake again. It meant that when I started running again I had lost all momentum. I saw them briefly at 11 miles and stopped again at just before halfway to do some *Breakfast* filming. Again I wasted another five minutes at least doing that and as I trundled over Tower Bridge I began to feel tired. Because I'd spent so much time messing around I was already going to be outside my target time of five and a half hours and mentally that suddenly hit me hard, as did the sight of hundreds of runners streaming the other way. They are the faster runners who have already completed the Isle of Dogs and are on the last four-mile stretch which again hits you like a train. I ran past the 14-mile marker in such a mood, I didn't notice it and it wasn't until I reached 15 miles that it really dawned on me how much

I was struggling. I called my husband tearfully and told him I was in a bad way. He encouraged me gently and told me to get to the next rendezvous point at 17 miles, where he would give me a hug and get me going again. The thing that struck me most was the realization that I still had 11 miles to go, I didn't feel great physically because it was so hot and hated everyone on the course who was standing outside pubs having a shandy shouting at the runners. I felt cross for putting myself through this and I just wanted it to be over. I knew I wouldn't back out, so I had no option but to get through this rough patch and pull myself together. But the self-doubt was crippling and when I look back at the whole experience, that is the battle that needs to be won. Physically I was okay – but mentally I was all over the shop.

I walked for a mile which didn't really help to be honest, so I started running again and limped to 17 miles. My husband and friends will never know how much they helped me. Just to hear them say, 'Christ you've already run 17 miles – bloody hell, well done!' really helped me through. It certainly did the trick because a mile later I was flying. From somewhere I found a new rhythm, got around the rest of the Isle of Dogs, which I believe is the toughest bit, and made the turn for home – which is massive psychologically. By the time I saw my support team again at 21 miles, I knew in my heart I was going to finish. The last five miles were a blur of excitement and emotion. By the time the Millennium Wheel hoved into view, I almost broke down. I knew I had won my battle, the culmination of months of hard work were going to have their reward. I was going to finish a marathon and I didn't want the race to end because I felt so fresh. I had definitely done enough training because I felt so good physically and was running past the stragglers. I phoned my husband to tell him I could see Big Ben and we were both tearful. By the time I got to Parliament Square I was almost sprinting I was so full of running and the last few hundred yards are the happiest I have ever known. Team Thearle were opposite Buckingham Palace and they went berserk when they saw me. I was talked home by the PA announcer, which meant I got a generous reception from the crowds of people who were still there. It was almost seven hours when I crossed the finish line, seven bloody hours. Paula Radcliffe could have been halfway to New York by the time I finished, but it didn't matter, I had finished. I did a quick television interview and then burst into grateful tears as my wonderful friends and family struck up a chorus of 'we love you Susie, we do'. I collected my bag, met Heather for a chat and a cry and then wandered to meet everyone at the appropriate meeting point where we drank champagne, took even more photos, I ate a giant mars bar and cried some more. My feet and body were fine, no blisters, no injuries, no nothing, just an aching tiredness that took a couple of days to go. But no problems at all. I had got my re-hydration strategy spot on, my race plan had worked and apart from my wedding day and the day Holly was born, I can honestly say I have never felt happier.

Whenever I talk about the marathon to people I inevitably cry. For me the battle is all mental and that's why it means so much to me. I truly believe anyone can run a marathon, I really do. I would never have believed I could do it, but I did. I am not a marathon runner and mentally I am someone who lacks confidence in my running ability because I'm not athletic. But I made myself do it and you can too. Willpower is the key, nothing more, nothing less. I refused to give in to the temptation of talking myself out of it and that victory of mind over body has had enormous implications in my life. It has freed me up to believe that anything is possible, because frankly it is. I know that my story has inspired others to run the race, because they have told me, including my husband, who danced around in about four hours a year later. When I add up the amount of time I wasted filming, chatting, taking photos etc, I reckon I actually did the distance in about 6 hours and 15 minutes. I have always sworn since that I would never do it again, but watching my husband train this year has made me feel slightly envious that I'm not doing it again. I still run, although eight miles is the furthest I have been since race day and although nothing will ever match that magical day when I lost my marathon virginity, I do secretly harbour a desire to do a sub-six-hour marathon. So will I do it again? Well, we'll see, because 26 miles is an awfully long way you know …

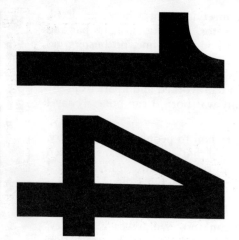

14

what next?

In this chapter you will learn:
- how to recover
- about the importance of having another goal
- why the timing of your new goal is crucial.

Tip at the top

It is quite likely that you will want another challenge soon after the marathon. Don't leave it until after that event to start planning. Do it beforehand!

From the minute that you signed up to your first marathon, right the way through your training and even on the start line all that you have been thinking about is getting to the finish – and rightly so! What about the next bit? What about your life afterwards?

Your life after the marathon could be a very different one from the one that you had before or it could go back to the same as before with the added bonus of some priceless memories that no-one can take away from you. It's up to you.

This is the opportunity to make some important changes in your life and many thousands of people each year fail to take it. The principal reason is that they don't think about life post marathon until after the event. That is wrong. You need to think about it before you start and make it a priority. Agreed, you have plenty to deal with now, but some serious thought now can make a serious difference to the years that follow.

Without sounding too dramatic, a marathon is truly a life-changing experience. It challenges you in a way that you have probably never experienced and it may well have produced a show of character that you didn't think you had. Once you have finished, the challenge is to take this onwards into other aspects of your life. They may not be physical challenges but instead social or mental challenges that you can similarly overcome. Once you have run a marathon you will feel you can conquer the world. Some forward planning will make that seem so much easier!

From the hours after the race to the months afterwards this chapter will explore what happens once you cross the finish line – one of the most emotional moments of your life.

The next three hours

As you round the final bend and see the finish you will experience a feeling like nothing you have ever gone through before. This is the culmination of months of hard work and hours of exhaustion, months of frustration and moments of doubt and sheer fear. There it is just ahead of you, the end of it all.

When you cross that line a number of things happen. First, there is the obvious elation, the overwhelming joy that you have achieved the goal that you set out to achieve back in the months of dark nights and torrential rain. Then comes the tiredness. Depending on your level of training this can lead to collapse or difficulty in walking. Perhaps just intense fatigue. As you exit the finish area, which can take some time in a big city-centre event like London or New York, you will probably still be suffering from a sense of disbelief. You will desperately want to see friends and family and share the moment with someone special. Remember that they have lived this unique experience and this moment belongs to them as well as you. Let them feel part of the occasion as you get swept up in the euphoria.

It takes time for these emotions to die down when you cross a marathon finish line for the first time and you need to be prepared for the intensity of it all. Tears might have been shed in the miles leading up to the finish line but if they haven't they may well be in the hours afterwards. They certainly will be by those in your support team and who can blame them. Remember their support in the dark days and make every effort you can to acknowledge the importance of the role that they have played. You may not have made it without them and you should never forget that.

As you get over that finish line, you should not forget – even though everyone around you will – to stretch. It will definitely not be on your list of priorities as you celebrate your achievements, but it should be. DOMS (Delayed Onset of Muscle Soreness), which will be covered later, is a condition from which many marathon runners suffer and if you stretch properly you could well offset its impact. Try and spend at least ten minutes stretching every muscle group and you will immediately feel the impact. You will have stretched after every one of your previous runs (or at least you should have done!), so why not now? You may struggle due to your feelings of fatigue, but do everything you can to make it happen. Ignore the strange looks from your fellow finishers and feel smug in the knowledge that you will probably feel better than them in the morning.

That night

Emotionally you will still feel incredibly drained the evening of the race, but by now your achievement will have sunk in. You may still be travelling back home but wherever you are you know you have done something very special. Your thoughts may well be turning to future challenges, but you will probably still be basking in the glory for many days to come.

Sleep may be harder to achieve than you imagine as your mind works overtime reliving every mile, every feeling of despair and every smile as you came down the home straight. Your body may be shattered but your mind probably won't let you sleep too well. You may not get to bed early as you relive all your memories to anyone around you who will listen!

The next day – marathon recovery

It is most likely that the next morning you will really appreciate what you have put your body through. You may pull back the covers and try and get out of bed as normal but you are likely to experience a common post-marathon problem: you can barely move! This is the world of Delayed Onset of Muscle Soreness, or DOMS.

DOMS is essentially stiffness of the muscles caused by exercise that the body is not accustomed to and for most people that includes running 26.2 miles! A number of factors are assumed to be contributory, including starvation of blood and oxygen to the muscles, the production of lactic acid and tears in the muscles themselves and/or connecting tissue.

Dealing with DOMS and therefore helping speed up the recovery process can be achieved through a combination of factors many of which are overlooked by the majority of runners. These include the stretching programme discussed above and the need to hydrate immediately after the run and over the next 24 hours. This is absolutely vital and again is ignored by many runners. Not only should you drink plenty of water but you should also eat plenty of carbohydrates to replenish your glycogen stores. These will have taken a real beating during the race and you need to get these back to normal levels as soon as possible to get your energy levels up where they were.

Muscle recovery can be aided by a massage as soon after the race as you can manage it and, if you can deal with it, a very cold bath within a few hours is a good idea.

The week after

The next seven days will be dominated by marathon talk. You will be in danger of telling everyone you meet your tales of the 26.2 miles, but don't let bored faces deter you – you deserve it! It's quite likely that your medal will barely leave your side – anyone who shows even the remotest level of interest will be shown your new pride and joy. Emotions will still be running high and you will still be struggling to believe that it is all over.

The tiredness and symptoms of DOMS will start to recede, but for a week at least you will be reminded hourly of what you have put your body through. Running a marathon is an extreme physical challenge and not something which that your body will recover from quickly. It takes many weeks to get over it properly so don't expect to tackle anything of similar magnitude for many weeks. Elite athletes aim to run only two or three marathons a year and for good reason – they would never be able to run at their best if they did not allow themselves sufficient recovery time. The same applies to those taking on their first marathon as the exertion levels are relative. Walking up and down stairs, running for a bus and pretty much anything that you take for granted will seem much more difficult than you might expect, but be patient and it will all get back to relative normality within a few days.

You may feel up to a light run by about Wednesday and if you do then it is to be recommended. It will help the recovery process and will help get you on the road to the next challenge. The longer you leave the first post-marathon run the tougher it will be. Don't overdo it though, as you may actually hinder the recovery if you try and do too much too soon.

By the end of the week you may be missing the training a little bit, although probably not too much! However, you may just be starting to feel that there is something missing.

The month after

After a week things start to change. If you have run on a guaranteed charity place the priority is now to collect the pledged sponsorship money and this can be a real challenge. Running the marathon will seem relatively straightforward if you have a few sponsors who won't pay up. Ideally you will have got most of the money up front but if you didn't then perseverance is the key. You've kept your side of the bargain; you need to make sure that sponsors keep theirs.

Interest in your marathon tales will start to diminish as time passes and although you will never forget it the memories will start to dim as the weeks pass.

Physically you will begin to feel much stronger as the month progresses and although running may still feel like hard work, by about the third week you will be able to run relatively comfortably, although you should not do excessive mileage.

If you haven't thought too much about your next challenge before it is likely that you will begin to do so during this month. For many runners doing a marathon means exactly that – doing one marathon and that's it. Although many think that from the outset, views can quickly change. Crossing that finish line is an experience that can affect people in many ways. Plenty say 'never again' while plenty more look forward to the next one, surprising themselves with their desire to do another. For many runners it is the intention from day one to treat the initial marathon as the first event on a fitness road that will encompass many differing challenges, including other running events like regular half marathons, triathlons or taking up a new sport.

It is of the utmost importance that you set your next target quickly or you may find that over the next few months you will drift away from fitness and your achievement becomes a distant memory replaced by nothing more than evenings in front of the TV. As outlined below, it is preferable that you start thinking about this before your first marathon rather than afterwards, but if you have left it late then do it as soon after the marathon as you can. The longer you leave it the harder it will be to achieve.

The importance of having another goal

Running a marathon is a major achievement and for many people it is a truly life-changing experience. It will be the start of a new chapter in their life. They have been challenged physically as never before and inevitably that can change anyone's outlook on life. Taking this impact and maximizing it can depend very much on what you do next. Obviously it is a good idea to have a decent rest, but without a clear goal for the future that rest can be permanent.

It is easy to be full of good intentions but far harder to plan for them and follow your marathon with another challenge that will ensure your fitness momentum is maintained. If you've no intention of doing anything similar ever again, no problem, but chances are that you will want to do something and probably quite soon. If you don't plan properly you will look back in a year's time when the weight has gone back on and be full of regret for a lost opportunity. There is an answer and that, as with most things, is thorough planning.

Throughout your marathon training you will be focusing only on the finish line, but it is important that you try to think beyond it and visualize what you would like to do afterwards. This is not easy as many days will be full of negative thoughts and the idea of doing anything beyond the marathon will be incomprehensible, but it is vital if you are to keep training once you complete the marathon.

In the weeks and months that follow your first marathon, putting your feet up for extended periods will seem a totally acceptable course of action. After too long, however, all your good work will be undone. If you have set another goal for fairly soon after the marathon you will keep training and the positive effects of the marathon will be amplified. It doesn't have to be a massive challenge. It could, for example, be a local half marathon, but it will keep you active and that is the purpose of setting goals early on. With a goal you will stay active but without one it is highly likely that you will not.

Each year many, many thousands of marathon runners step over the finish line and hang up their running shoes both intentionally and as a result of poor planning. Intentions may have been high to do other things but it all came to nothing. Before long their fitness has gone and with it a chance to get more out of life.

For thousands of others crossing that line is the start of something much bigger. For them it is a life-changing experience that opens the door to so much more. The majority of this group will know what's next before they even get to the start line and that is what you must do. Get planning for your fitness future now.

Which of these two groups do you want to join?

Your next marathon

If you are one of the many thousands who decide that the first marathon should be followed by another then you must think carefully about the next one and plan accordingly.

The best five marathons in the world, known collectively as the World Marathon Majors are London, Boston, Berlin, Chicago and New York and if you do one of these as your first then doing one of the others will ensure a similar experience. Do one outside of this group and your experience may not be as memorable. Sure, there are plenty of excellent marathons worldwide but there are few that are as well organized or as well supported. It is this point which is particularly important. Running your first marathon in a mass participation event like London will raise your expectations levels. You will assume that all races of this type have similarly massive crowds but they most definitely do not. Many will seem so at the start but after a few kilometres they will virtually disappear and you will feel as if you are on your own.

The value of a big crowd cannot be underestimated. Many marathon runners insist that a vociferous crowd can carry them through the final six miles with its screaming, cheering and, if you have your name on your vest, incredible personal support. If one of the World Marathon Majors is your first race then you will take this support for granted and it can come as a nasty shock if it is not there in your next event.

Think carefully about your next race and if it is a big city-centre marathon that you want – and it would be recommended for your second race – then you will need to get it booked early. You will find it very difficult to finish London, for example, and expect to get into any of the other majors unless you secure a guaranteed place through a charity. Have a look at realbuzz.com for more on the majors and how you can get one of these charity places. The majors are all extremely popular events and all sell out quickly so you must enter as soon as you can. Don't wait until you have finished one before entering another. Plan a schedule and book them all early. You may think it's a bit optimistic entering your second and third marathons before you've even run your first one. It's not. It's just good planning and it will ensure that everything that you have gained from your first will not be lost. You will keep your fitness and the 'can do' attitude that is so evident in so many marathon runners.

If you think that one big city-centre race is enough and you want to do something different then there is plenty of choice. Again, though, you must plan ahead. Some of them you will be able to enter pretty late on, but some can be booked out many, many months ahead. Unique events like the Antarctica Marathon, Great Wall of China Marathon and Everest Marathon take small groups and they are part of organized tour packages so you must get involved up to a year ahead if you think something like this is for you. It may be a bit ambitious to go for events like these too soon, but they are well worth looking at after you have a few more 'traditional' races under your belt. Think about one of the European races like Prague, Stockholm or the Midnight Sun Marathon in Tromso, which starts at midnight in bright sunshine! These events all give you great memories but remember, don't expect too much support out on the course!

If you live in the UK it is worth remembering that no marathon comes remotely close to the Flora London Marathon in any respect. It is well and truly unique and if you do decide to try one of the other marathons on offer then you should expect a completely different experience. Some of them will be two or three laps around a rural circuit, some will offer the promise of a city-centre route only to take you into the countryside for much of it and with all of them there will be virtually no-one watching and that is not an exaggeration. London is the only event in the UK which brings residents and visitors alike onto the streets. No other domestic event even comes close.

If you are in the US clearly New York, Boston and Chicago are in a class of their own, but there are plenty of others that offer good organization, big fields and significant crowds. Try these three first though before venturing elsewhere.

Whichever race you go for as your second event, remember that it will be a very different experience all round from your first. Being a virgin marathoner is something special and although this may imply that the second isn't as good, it means that it will be different. It doesn't matter how many times you run over a marathon finishing line however, it still feels great!

taking it further

To find out more about running a marathon check out the running section of **www.realbuzz.com**. Realbuzz.com has a growing number of pages on sports, health and fitness, diet and nutrition, the great outdoors, travel, entertainment, and charity adventures. Users can meet like-minded people, share recommendations and stories, and discuss their favourite pastimes – all online. As the online partner to the Flora London Marathon, The BUPA Great North Run and the World Marathon Majors you can be sure you will find all the help and support that you need, including an extensive race calendar, to make your marathon day one that you will never forget.

Have a look at **www.worldmarathonmajors.com** for information on all of the big five marathons and **www.london-marathon.co.uk** for the latest on the Flora London Marathon, including how to enter. The site also contains a list of approved physiotherapy clinics.

To run for a charity in this great race go to the Charity Places section. The official charity in the 2007 Flora London Marathon is WellChild and they have plenty of guaranteed entries. Check out **www.realbuzz.com/microsites/wellchild/index.php** for more information. In 2006 the official charities were The Anthony Nolan Trust **www.realbuzz.com/microsites/anthony_nolan/index.php**. and The Stroke Association **www.stroke.org.uk/**. If you'd like to join Sue Thearle and run for the Help the Hospices check out **www.hospicerunners.org.uk**.

Two other charities to look out for are Children with Leukaemia **www.runleukaemia.org** and Cancer Research UK **www.cancerresearchuk.org/running/**.

For all your kit needs head to the London Marathon Store at 63 Long Acre, Covent Garden, London, WC2E 9JN. Or call 020 7240 1244 or go online at **www.londonmarathonstore.com**.

teach
yourself

fitness
jeff archer

- Do you want to get fit?
- Do you need to know how to make exercise part of daily life?
- Would you like to set and reach physical goals?

Can't find the time to get fit? Don't know where to start? **Fitness** will show you how to formulate, set and stick to a realistic exercise routine, whatever your age or ability. Covering everything from staying motivated to eating sensibly and avoiding injury, this book will help you to stay fit with or without a gym, and even with the family. Featuring exercises, information, tips and tricks, this is all you need to get fit and stay that way.

Jeff Archer is a personal trainer and life coach, and a founder and director of The Tonic, a lifestyle and fitness consultancy – www.the-tonic.com.

teach yourself ®

From Advanced Sudoku to Zulu, you'll find everything you need in the **teach yourself** range, in books, on CD and on DVD.

Visit **www.teachyourself.co.uk** for more details.

Advanced Sudoku & Kakuro
Afrikaans
Alexander Technique
Algebra
Ancient Greek
Applied Psychology
Arabic
Aromatherapy
Art History
Astrology
Astronomy
AutoCAD 2004
AutoCAD 2007
Ayurveda
Baby Massage and Yoga
Baby Signing
Baby Sleep
Bach Flower Remedies
Backgammon
Ballroom Dancing
Basic Accounting
Basic Computer Skills
Basic Mathematics
Beauty
Beekeeping
Beginner's Arabic Script
Beginner's Chinese
Beginner's Chinese Script

Beginner's Dutch
Beginner's French
Beginner's German
Beginner's Greek
Beginner's Greek Script
Beginner's Hindi
Beginner's Italian
Beginner's Japanese
Beginner's Japanese Script
Beginner's Latin
Beginner's Portuguese
Beginner's Russian
Beginner's Russian Script
Beginner's Spanish
Beginner's Turkish
Beginner's Urdu Script
Bengali
Better Bridge
Better Chess
Better Driving
Better Handwriting
Biblical Hebrew
Biology
Birdwatching
Blogging
Body Language
Book Keeping
Brazilian Portuguese

Bridge
Buddhism
Bulgarian
Business Chinese
Business French
Business Japanese
Business Plans
Business Spanish
Business Studies
Buying a Home in France
Buying a Home in Italy
Buying a Home in Portugal
Buying a Home in Spain
C++
Calculus
Calligraphy
Cantonese
Car Buying and Maintenance
Card Games
Catalan
Chess
Chi Kung
Chinese Medicine
Chinese
Christianity
Classical Music
Coaching
Collecting
Computing for the Over 50s
Consulting
Copywriting
Correct English
Counselling
Creative Writing
Cricket
Croatian
Crystal Healing
CVs
Czech
Danish
Decluttering
Desktop Publishing
Detox
Digital Photography
Digital Video & PC Editing

Dog Training
Drawing
Dream Interpretation
Dutch
Dutch Conversation
Dutch Dictionary
Dutch Grammar
Eastern Philosophy
Electronics
English as a Foreign Language
English for International
    Business
English Grammar
English Grammar as a Foreign
    Language
English Vocabulary
Entrepreneurship
Estonian
Ethics
Excel 2003
Feng Shui
Film Making
Film Studies
Finance for Non-Financial
    Managers
Finnish
Fitness
Flash 8
Flash MX
Flexible Working
Flirting
Flower Arranging
Franchising
French
French Conversation
French Dictionary
French Grammar
French Phrasebook
French Starter Kit
French Verbs
French Vocabulary
Freud
Gaelic
Gardening
Genetics

Geology
German
German Conversation
German Grammar
German Phrasebook
German Verbs
German Vocabulary
Globalization
Go
Golf
Good Study Skills
Great Sex
Greek
Greek Conversation
Greek Phrasebook
Growing Your Business
Guitar
Gulf Arabic
Hand Reflexology
Hausa
Herbal Medicine
Hieroglyphics
Hindi
Hinduism
Home PC Maintenance and
 Networking
How to DJ
How to Run a Marathon
How to Win at Casino Games
How to Win at Horse Racing
How to Win at Online Gambling
How To Win At Poker
How to Write A Blockbuster
Human Anatomy & Physiology
Hungarian
Icelandic
Improve Your French
Improve Your German
Improve Your Italian
Improve Your Spanish
Improving your Employability
Indian Head Massage
Indonesian
Instant French
Instant German
Instant Greek

Instant Italian
Instant Japanese
Instant Portuguese
Instant Russian
Instant Spanish
Irish
Irish Conversation
Irish Grammar
Islam
Italian
Italian Conversation
Italian Grammar
Italian Phrasebook
Italian Starter Kit
Italian Verbs
Italian Vocabulary
Japanese
Japanese Conversation
Java
JavaScript
Jazz
Jewellery Making
Judaism
Jung
Keeping a Rabbit
Keeping Aquarium Fish
Keeping Pigs
Keeping Poultry
Knitting
Korean
Latin American Spanish
Latin
Latin Dictionary
Latin Grammar
Latvian
Letter Writing Skills
Life at 50: For Men
Life at 50: For Women
Life Coaching
Linguistics
LINUX
Lithuanian
Magic
Mahjong
Malay
Managing Stress

Managing Your Own Career
Mandarin Chinese Conversation
Marketing
Marx
Massage
Mathematics
Meditation
Modern China
Modern Hebrew
Modern Persian
Mosaics
Music Theory
Mussolini's Italy
Nazi Germany
Negotiating
Nepali
New Testament Greek
NLP
Norwegian
Norwegian Conversation
Old English
One-Day French
One-Day French - the DVD
One-Day German
One-Day Greek
One-Day Italian
One-Day Portuguese
One-Day Spanish
One-Day Spanish - the DVD
Origami
Owning a Cat
Owning A Horse
Panjabi
PC Networking for Small
  Businesses
Personal Safety and Self
  Defence
Philosophy
Philosophy of Mind
Philosophy of Religion
Photography
Photoshop
PHP with MySQL
Physics
Piano

Pilates
Planning Your Wedding
Polish
Polish Conversation
Politics
Portuguese
Portuguese Conversation
Portuguese Grammar
Portuguese Phrasebook
Postmodernism
Pottery
PowerPoint 2003
PR
Project Management
Psychology
Quick Fix French Grammar
Quick Fix German Grammar
Quick Fix Italian Grammar
Quick Fix Spanish Grammar
Quick Fix: Access 2002
Quick Fix: Excel 2000
Quick Fix: Excel 2002
Quick Fix: HTML
Quick Fix: Windows XP
Quick Fix: Word
Quilting
Recruitment
Reflexology
Reiki
Relaxation
Retaining Staff
Romanian
Running Your Own Business
Russian
Russian Conversation
Russian Grammar
Sage Line 50
Sanskrit
Screenwriting
Serbian
Setting Up A Small Business
Shorthand Pitman 2000
Sikhism
Singing
Slovene

Small Business Accounting
Small Business Health Check
Songwriting
Spanish
Spanish Conversation
Spanish Dictionary
Spanish Grammar
Spanish Phrasebook
Spanish Starter Kit
Spanish Verbs
Spanish Vocabulary
Speaking On Special Occasions
Speed Reading
Stalin's Russia
Stand Up Comedy
Statistics
Stop Smoking
Sudoku
Swahili
Swahili Dictionary
Swedish
Swedish Conversation
Tagalog
Tai Chi
Tantric Sex
Tap Dancing
Teaching English as a Foreign
    Language
Teams & Team Working
Thai
The British Empire
The British Monarchy from
    Henry VIII
The Cold War
The First World War
The History of Ireland
The Internet
The Kama Sutra
The Middle East Since 1945
The Second World War
Theatre
Time Management
Tracing Your Family History
Training
Travel Writing

Trigonometry
Turkish
Turkish Conversation
Twentieth Century USA
Typing
Ukrainian
Understanding Tax for Small
    Businesses
Understanding Terrorism
Urdu
Vietnamese
Visual Basic
Volcanoes
Watercolour Painting
Weight Control through Diet &
    Exercise
Welsh
Welsh Dictionary
Welsh Grammar
Wills & Probate
Windows XP
Wine Tasting
Winning at Job Interviews
Word 2003
World Cultures: China
World Cultures: England
World Cultures: Germany
World Cultures: Italy
World Cultures: Japan
World Cultures: Portugal
World Cultures: Russia
World Cultures: Spain
World Cultures: Wales
World Faiths
Writing a Novel
Writing Crime Fiction
Writing for Children
Writing for Magazines
Writing Poetry
Xhosa
Yiddish
Yoga
Zen
Zulu